AQA
PSYCHOLOGY
For A Level
Year 1 & AS

Revision Guide

2nd Ed

Cara Flanagan

Michael Griffin

Matt Jarvis

Rob Liddle

Illuminate
Publishing

Published in 2020 by Illuminate Publishing Ltd,
P.O. Box 1160, Cheltenham, Gloucestershire GL50 9RW

Orders: Please visit www.illuminatepublishing.com
or email sales@illuminatepublishing.com

British Library Cataloguing in Publication Data

A catalogue record for this book is available from the
British Library

ISBN 978-1-912820-43-6

Printed in the UK by Cambrian Printers, Aberystwyth
03.21

The publisher's policy is to use papers that are natural,
renewable and recyclable products made from
wood grown in sustainable forests. The logging and
manufacturing processes are expected to conform to the
environmental regulations of the country of origin.

Every effort has been made to contact copyright holders
of material produced in this book. If notifed, the publisher
will be pleased to rectify any errors or omissions at the
earliest opportunity.

Editor: Nic Watson

Cover design: Nigel Harriss

Text design: Nigel Harriss

Layout: Sarah Clifford

Front cover photographer: Jason Duda

Model: Madeline Rae Mason

Acknowledgements:

p.10, 16, 18, 32, 36, 38, 44, 90, 96, 115, 122 © Illuminate Publishing

p.73 © Craig Swanson www.perspicuity.com

p.3 and 128 stars Aha-Soft / Shutterstock.com; p.5 marekuliasz /
Shutterstock.com; Aleksova / Shutterstock.com; Sashkin / Shutterstock.
com; p.6 Kuklos / Shutterstock.com; p.7 ostill / Shutterstock.com;
p.11 fizkes / Shutterstock.com; p.12 Baronb / Shutterstock.com;
p.13 lexaarts / Shutterstock.com; p.14 Fer Gregory / Shutterstock.com;
p.15 sirtravelalot / Shutterstock.com; p.17 alphaspirit / Shutterstock.com;
p.18 Asier Romero / Shutterstock.com; p.19 sirtravelalot / Shutterstock.
com; p.20 ESB Professional / Shutterstock.com; p.21 pixelheadphoto
digitalskillet / Shutterstock.com; p.22 Quick Shot / Shutterstock.com;
p.23 Massimo Todaro / Shutterstock.com; p.24 Nikita Vishneveckiy /
Shutterstock.com; p.25 GoodStudio / Shutterstock.com; p.26 Peter
Gudella / Shutterstock.com; p.27 Pixeljoy / Shutterstock.com; p.27
Peter Gudella / Shutterstock.com; p.28 seahorsetwo / Shutterstock.
com; p.29 Both stockphoto-graf / Shutterstock.com; p.30 Max Bukovski
/ Shutterstock.com; p.31 pathdoc / Shutterstock.com; p.32 Frank
Gaertner / Shutterstock.com; p.34 ESB Professional / Shutterstock.
com; p.35 Monkey Business Images / Shutterstock.com; p.37 pathdoc
/ Shutterstock.com; p.38 Vikafoto33 / Shutterstock.com; p.39 Ollyy
/ Shutterstock.com; p.40 ER_09 / Shutterstock.com; MaryValery
/ Shutterstock.com; p.41 Jesada Sabai / Shutterstock.com; p.42
Igorusha / Shutterstock.com; p.43 Twin Design / Shutterstock.com; p.45
wickerwood / Shutterstock.com; p.46 Brian A Jackson / Shutterstock.
com; p.47 Photographee.eu / Shutterstock.com; p.48 Monkey Business
Images; p.49 Mila Supinskaya Glashchenko / Shutterstock.com; p.50
DGLimages / Shutterstock.com; p.51 Liashenko Olga / Shutterstock.
com; p.52 Olesia Bilkei / Shutterstock.com; p.53 fotofeel / Shutterstock.
com; p.54 Tinseltown / Shutterstock.com; SCIENCE SOURCE/SCIENCE
PHOTO LIBRARY; kathmanduphotog / Shutterstock.com; p.56 alice-
photo / Shutterstock.com; p.57 IVASHstudio / Shutterstock.com; p.58
RimDream / Shutterstock.com; p.59 VGstockstudio / Shutterstock.
com; p.60 Rasulov / Shutterstock.com; p.61 Monkey Business Images /
Shutterstock.com; p.62 Feel Photo Art / Shutterstock.com; p.63 Sarah
Noda / Shutterstock.com; p.64 topten22photo / Shutterstock.com;
p.65 adriaticfoto / Shutterstock.com; p.66 Radiokafka / Shutterstock.
com; p.67 Ocskay Bence / Shutterstock.com; p.68 Rawpixel.com /
Shutterstock.com; p.69 Kaspars Grinvalds / Shutterstock.com; p.70
CYCLONEPROJECT / Shutterstock.com; p.72 WilleeCole Photography /
Shutterstock.com; p.74 bbernard / Shutterstock.com; p.75 valeriya_sh /
Shutterstock.com; p.77 Lukiyanova Natalia / frenta / Shutterstock.com;
p.78 Katrina Elena / Shutterstock.com; p.79 klss / Shutterstock.com;
p.81 Mike Baldwin / Cornered; p.82 Fotolia; p.83 joshya / Shutterstock.
com; p.84 RACOBOVT / Shutterstock.com; p.85 Nantz / Shutterstock.
com; p.86 Volodimir Zozulinskyi / Shutterstock.com; p.87 Joseph
Sohm / Shutterstock.com; p.88 arda savasciogullari / Shutterstock.
com; p.89 wavebreakmedia / Shutterstock.com; p.90 Lightspring /
Shutterstock.com; p.92 yochika photographer / Shutterstock.com;
p.93 Brocreative / Shutterstock.com; p.94 fizkes / Shutterstock.com;
p.95 vchal / Shutterstock.com, Oriol Domingo / Shutterstock.com;
p.97 Photographee.eu / Shutterstock.com; p.98 Zastolskiy Victor /
Shutterstock.com; p.99 PathDoc / Shutterstock.com; p.100 Twin Design
/ Shutterstock.com; p.101 Chirawan Thaiprasansap / Shutterstock.com;
p.102 SoRad / Shutterstock.com; p.103 rdrgraphe / Shutterstock.com;
p.104 MJTH / Shutterstock.com; p.105 Guayo Fuentes / Shutterstock.
com; airdone / Shutterstock.com; Just dance / Shutterstock.com; p.106
pirke / Shutterstock.com; p.107 Melica / Shutterstock.com; p.109 Vitalinka
/ Shutterstock.com; p.110 ArtOfPhotos / Shutterstock.com; p.111 BeRad /
Shutterstock.com; p.112 Anna.zabella / Shutterstock.com; p.113 PathDoc
/ Shutterstock.com; p.115 Big Joe / Shutterstock.com; p.116 John T Takai
/ Shutterstock.com; p.117 Kjpargeter / Shutterstock.com; p.118 G-Stock
Studio / Shutterstock.com; p.120 Iakov Kalinin / Shutterstock.com.

Unsung heroes

This wonderful little book is the product of the
four authors but we owe considerable gratitude to
Dr Tracey Elder who helped ensure the questions
in the book reflect assessment practice; Arwa
Mohamedbhai for writing the suggested answers to
the Knowledge Check feature (see p.6 for details) and
above all those who manage the whole production –
first of all our mentor and most wonderful publisher,
Rick Jackman and the very special team at Illuminate
(Clare Jackman, Peter Burton and Saskia Burton).

Second to Nigel Harriss, supreme designer, who is
responsible for the unique and spectacular design,
and Sarah Clifford who has gone above and
beyond in working wonders adapting the design
where needed and getting all our material to fit
on the page.

And finally to Nic Watson who is our editor but that
doesn't begin to describe what she does – she has
our backs and makes sure that everything that needs
to be checked is checked, and does all of this with
enormous patience, kindness and fanatical attention
to detail.

About the authors

Cara is author of many books for A level students and a conference
organiser and speaker; she is also senior editor of *Psychology Review*.
She is looking forward to spending more time lying on a beach or
climbing mountains.

Michael is a teacher of psychology, Assistant Headteacher and
previous Head of Sixth Form. He is an author of resources for the
delivery of psychology lessons and provides CPD for other psychology
teachers.

Matt is a Chartered Psychologist and Associate Fellow of the British
Psychological Society. He taught psychology for 25 years and is
currently Learning Technology and Innovation Manager for a Social
Justice and Education charity. Matt is also an editor of *Psychology
Review*. When not working or writing Matt DJs and loves live music
and festivals.

Rob was an A level teacher for more than 20 years and would like to
give a big shout out to his ex-colleagues at Winstanley College. In his
spare moments, he likes nothing more than to pluck away tunelessly
at his guitar, ideally in the Lake District. He plans to ask Matt how you
become a Chartered Psychologist. In an eerie echo of the first edition
of this book, he still hasn't seen *Frozen 2*.

Contents

For a free download of suggested answers to the Knowledge Check feature visit www.illuminatepublishing.com/2edpsychrganswers1

Revision Guides

Flashbooks

Revision Apps

=

An unbeatable combination for revision!
Visit www.illuminatepublishing.com/aqapsych

Introduction

AO stands for 'assessment objective'.

Apply it

The 'Apply it' questions throughout this book aim to help you practise AO2 skills – about 30% of the marks in the exam are AO2.

The exam papers are divided into sections (Section A, Section B, etc).

In Section A on Paper 1 there are questions on Social influence and Section B is on Memory – but the *type* of question is unpredictable. You might have an essay question and/or there may be research methods questions and/or an application question. There is no pattern to the way the types of questions are distributed in the exam.

Research methods questions will be in every section in addition to the Research methods section on Paper 2.

Types of exam questions

AO1	Define, outline, describe, explain	Explain what is meant by 'obedience'. (*2 marks*)
		Outline **one** emotional characteristic of depression. (*2 marks*)
		In relation to social learning theory, explain what 'modelling' means. (*4 marks*)
AO2	Application	[Stem] Tulisa has started at a new school and notices that all the girls are wearing long skirts. She doesn't want to be different and wants them to like her, so the next day she wears a long skirt, too.
		[Question] Explain which type of conformity Tulisa is showing. Explain your decision. (*3 marks*)
AO3	One strength/ limitation	Outline **one** limitation of the multi-store model. (*2 marks*)
	Evaluation	Evaluate Bowlby's monotropic theory of attachment. (*6 marks*)
AO1 + AO3	Mini-essays	Discuss research into conformity. (*8 marks*)
	Extended writing	Outline **and** evaluate a dispositional explanation for obedience. (*12 marks AS, 16 marks AL*)
		Describe **and** evaluate Romanian orphan studies. (*12 marks AS, 16 marks AL*)
AO1 + AO2 + AO3	Extended writing + applications	[Stem] Maria recently failed her driving test. She says the test was unfair and the examiner was 'out to get her'. She says she hates herself and will never try anything again. Before the test Maria told her friend that she had to pass otherwise she could not go on. Maria's friend thinks she might be showing signs of depression.
		[Question] Describe **and** evaluate the cognitive approach to explaining depression. Refer to Maria in your answer. (*12 marks AS, 16 marks AL*)

About 25% of the marks for your AS exam will come from questions on research methods.

Research methods questions

AO1	Explain	Explain what is meant by a 'behavioural category'. (*2 marks*)
AO2	Application	[Stem] Participants were given a list of organised and unorganised words and their recall was tested.
		[Question] Explain how randomisation could have been used in this experiment. (*2 marks*)
AO3	Evaluate	Explain **one** strength of an independent groups design. (*2 marks*)

What to do for a Grade A

Top class AO1	Top class AO1 ... includes details and specialist terms. For example: • This is good → Milgram (in the 1960s) described the agentic state as an explanation ... • This isn't good → One study found people obeyed someone who was in charge... You don't need to write more, you just need to include specific bits of information such as specialist terms, researcher's names, percentages and so on.
Top class AO2	Top class AO2 ... uses text or quotes from the stem of the question. For example: • This is good → Tulisa is showing normative social influence because she wears a long skirt so she is like the others and they will like her. • This isn't good → One type of conformity is normative which is wanting to be liked, like Tulisa. It's not enough to just mention a few key words – you must really engage with the stem. This is a skill that needs practice.

Top class AO3	Top class AO3 ... is elaborated and therefore effective. For example:
	❶ **Beginner** level: State your **point**: One limitation is ... This theory is supported by ... One strength is ....
	❷ **Intermediate** level: Add some **context**.
	  • This is good → One limitation is that artificial materials were used. The study by the Petersons used consonant syllables.
	  • This isn't good → One limitation is that artificial materials were used. This doesn't tell us about everyday life.
	    The second example is generic – it could be used anywhere.
	    Context is king.
	❸ **Higher** level: Add further **explanation** to make the point **thorough** or add a **counterpoint.**
	❹ Finish with a **conclusion** e.g. 'This shows that ...'
	    Read the evaluations throughout this book as examples of expert level.
	If you find higher level difficult then just do intermediate. In an AS essay aim to do three intermediate evaluations and that should get you the full 6 marks. In an A level essay two intermediate and two higher points is probably OK for 10 marks.
	Whatever you do AVOID a list of beginner level evaluations.

Top class essays	Make it organised – it helps the examiner see the separate elements of your answer. Use paragraphs. There is more advice on essay (extended writing) questions on the next page ...

Describe **FEWER** studies but describe them in detail.

Identify **FEWER** critical points, but explain each one thoroughly.

ALL I WANT FOR CHRISTMAS

List-like is bad.

It's actually quite easy to list lots of points – explaining them is challenging.

Context is king

Good evaluation points must contain evidence.

Your point may be well-elaborated but, if the same elaborated point can be placed in many different essays then it is too **EASY**.

Good evaluation points must have **CONTEXT**.

Exam advice

The term 'research' refers to theories, explanations or studies.

Knowledge Check

The Knowledge Check questions throughout this book should help you identify many of the different ways that questions will be asked in the exam.

On the AS paper there are 72 marks and it is a 90-minute exam, which gives you 1¼ minutes for each mark.

On A level papers there are 96 marks and it is a 120-minute exam which also gives you 1¼ minutes for each mark.

Just because you have written lots doesn't mean you will get high marks.

Students who write a long answer often do poorly.

- It may not answer the question.
- Spending too much time on one question means less time elsewhere.
- Your answer may lack detail – lists of studies and lists of critical points don't get high marks.
- Long essays are often very descriptive and there are never more than 6 marks for description.

Download suggested answers to the Knowledge Check questions from **tinyurl.com/y8kjyvwe**

More information if you can bear it

There are lots of little rules

One or more Two or more	Describe **one or more** explanations of obedience. *(6 marks)*
	This means you can potentially gain full marks for just one explanation (this gives you time to describe and evaluate it fully, which is important to show detail).
	Or you can elect to do more explanations – but too many explanations is not good because your answer becomes list-like (no details and no elaboration).
Distinguish between	Explain the difference between insecure–resistant and insecure–avoidant attachment types. *(4 marks)*
	The danger is that you will simply describe each item. You must find a way to contrast them both, for example considering how each attachment type responds to stranger anxiety.
Essays with extra information	Discuss the behaviourist approach. Refer to research studies in your answers. *(12 marks)*
	Describe **one** animal study of attachment. Include details of what the researcher(s) did and what they found. *(4 marks)*
	Make sure you satisfy the demands of ALL parts of the question.

How much should I write?

	In general 25–30 words per mark is a good rule – as long as the answer is focused on the topic.
	For an AS essay of 12 marks you might therefore write:
	AO1 150–200 words AO3 150–200 words
	For an AL essay of 16 marks you might therefore write:
	AO1 150–200 words AO3 250–300 words

Here are two ways to produce top class AS essays:

Route 1	**Route 2**
6 marks AO1	*6 marks AO1*
Six paragraphs/points, write about 150 words.	*Six* paragraphs/points, write about 150 words.
6 marks AO3	*6 marks AO3*
Three paragraphs/evaluations at *intermediate level*, write about 150 words.	*Two* paragraphs/evaluations at *higher level*. Doing just two gives you time to elaborate more. Write about 150 words.

Effective revision

Create revision cards.	For **description** the maximum you need is about 150 words.

- Identify 6–8 points on the topic.
- Record a trigger phrase in left-hand column.
- Record about 25–30 words in right-hand column.

For example

AO1 Key point	Description
Locus of control (LOC)	Rotter suggested people have a sense of what controls their behaviour.
Internals	Some people believe that the things that happen to them are largely controlled by themselves. For example, if you do well in an exam it is because you worked hard.
Externals	Other people believe that things happen without their control. If they did well in an exam they might say it was good luck or the textbook. If they fail it was bad luck or the questions were hard.

Reduce your cards to the minimum.

Cue words	Description
Rotter LOC	A sense of what controls your behaviour.
Internal	Own control, e.g. poor exam mark due to lack of effort.
External	Outside our control, e.g. bad luck, bad teacher.

For **evaluation** the maximum you need for AS extended writing questions is about 150 words.

- Identify 2–3 critical points (remember LESS IS MORE).
- Record a trigger phrase in left-hand column.
- For intermediate level, record evidence in the next column.
- For higher level add some further evidence.
- You should add a conclusion when you write out the whole point, for example 'This shows that ...'. Look at the conclusions we have written in this book – they start with 'This' or 'Therefore'.

For example

AO3 Key point	Intermediate level evaluation	Higher level evaluation
There is research support.	Holland measured levels of LOC in a repeat of Milgram's study. 37% of internals did not continue whereas only 23% of externals did not continue.	So internals showed a greater level of resistance than externals.

Rehearse the content.	Cover up the right-hand column and try to recall what is there using the trigger phrase.
Rehearse the trigger phrases.	When you are standing at a bus stop, see if you can remember all the trigger words for one topic.
Practise writing timed answers	Write an essay answer with your trigger card in front of you. Give yourself 15 minutes for a 12-mark answer. Give yourself 20 minutes for a 16-mark answer.

If you learn too much you will just try to squeeze it into the exam and you don't have time.

Focus on fewer points and make sure you explain them in detail. That's where the marks are.

In this book we have provided 6 points of AO1 for each topic, consisting of a trigger word/phrase and explanations. For example on page 32 you will find the following AO1 (descriptive) content:

Separate memory stores.	The MSM describes how information flows through the memory system. Memory is made of three stores linked by processing.
Sensory register (SR).	All stimuli from the environment (e.g. the sound of someone talking) pass into the SR. This part of memory is not one store but five, one for each sense. • Coding – modality-specific, depends on the sense (visual in iconic, acoustic in echoic, etc.). • Duration – very brief, less than half a second (see research on facing page). • Capacity – very high, e.g. over one hundred million cells in one eye, each storing data.
Transfer from SR to STM.	Information passes further into memory only if attention is paid to it (attention is the key process).
Short-term memory (STM).	A limited capacity store of temporary duration. • Coding – acoustic (based on sound). • Duration – about 18 seconds unless the information is rehearsed. • Capacity – between 5 and 9 (7 ± 2) items before some forgetting occurs (Cowan argues for around 5).
Transfer from STM to LTM.	Maintenance rehearsal occurs when we repeat (rehearse) material to ourselves. We can keep information in STM as long as we rehearse it. If we rehearse it long enough, it passes into LTM.
Long-term memory (LTM).	A permanent memory store. • Coding – mostly semantic (i.e. in terms of meaning). • Duration – potentially up to a lifetime. • Capacity – potentially unlimited.
Retrieval from LTM.	When we want to recall information stored in LTM it has to be transferred back to STM by a process called retrieval.

No athlete would dream of running a race without doing many practice runs of the right distance and within a set time.

Understanding marking

AO1 question: Outline the procedure used in one study of animal attachment. *(4 marks)*

Answer Harlow's study was with baby monkeys. He had observed that baby monkeys often survived better in cages without their mother if you gave them a soft cloth to cuddle. He set up an experiment to test this where there were two wire mothers. In one condition, one of the mothers had a feeding bottle attached while the other one was covered in cloth. The monkeys were kept all the time in a cage just with these two wire mothers. The monkeys spent their time with the cloth-covered mother not the other one, which shows that contact comfort is important in attachment. (103 words)

AO2 question: Some friends are planning what they might do at the weekend. Most of them want to try out a new nightclub. But Sam fancies going to see a band he likes instead.

Briefly explain how each of the factors of group size, unanimity and task difficulty might influence whether or not Sam conforms to the majority. *(6 marks)*

Answer Sam is likely to conform if more than three of his friends want to go to the new club. Asch found, in his research, that levels of conformity rose up to having three confederates but it didn't get more after that. So a majority of three is probably enough – but in Asch's research that led to 32% conformity so Sam might still not conform.

If one of his friends decided not to go to the club then Sam might feel more likely to dissent too. Asch found that even if the dissenter gave a different answer from the real participant this was enough to break the conformity. So Sam might go to see the band even if the dissenting friend wasn't going to do that either.

In terms of task difficulty it sounds like the band is something he knows well (a band he likes) whereas the nightclub is new and a less safe option which makes it a difficult decision. Asch found that conformity rose when people had to make judgements that were more difficult so Sam might just conform. (187 words)

AO3 question: Briefly evaluate learning theory as an explanation of attachment. *(4 marks)*

Answer Learning theory is the behaviourist explanation of attachment, based on classical and operant conditioning. Harlow's study with monkeys showed that this explanation was wrong. In this study, in one condition, baby monkeys had a choice of a wire mother with a feeding bottle or one covered in cloth. They chose the one covered in cloth. This shows that attachment is not related to feeding as the behaviourists predicted.

Another limitation of the learning theory of attachment is that it is only focused on behaviour and does not include other factors that may influence attachment, such as interactional synchrony. (100 words)

Examiner comments

Level	Marks	Knowledge	Clarity and organisation	Coherence	Specialist terminology
2	3–4	Some detail, accurate	Clear ✔	Coherent ✔	Effective use
1	1–2	Limited ✔	Lacking	Lacking	Absent or inappropriate ✔
	0	No relevant content			

Comments The first two sentences contribute nothing and the final sentence is on findings. That leaves some fairly limited description about the methods. The answer is mostly accurate but lacks clarity because of the irrelevant material. There is a lack of specialist terminology. Level 1, towards the top. *2 marks.*

Level	Marks	Knowledge	Application	Effectiveness	Clarity and coherence	Specialist terminology
3	5–6	Well-detailed	Clear ✔	Effective ✔	Generally coherent ✔	Appropriate
2	3–4	Evident ✔	Evident	Some effectiveness	Sometimes lacking	On occasions
1	1–2	Inaccuracies	Limited	Limited	Lacking	Absent or inappropriate ✔
	0	No relevant content				

Comments A thorough answer where the student has focused very clearly on the stem at the beginning of each paragraph and linked this to Asch's research.

With reference to the mark scheme we can see that the level of knowledge is clear and reasonably well-detailed – more so in the first paragraph. In the other paragraphs some finer details of the research are missing.

The application is mostly clear and effective. The student has gone beyond simply mentioning 'Sam' in that there are references to the new nightclub and the band he likes.

The answer is coherent but not effective in use of terminology.

Level 3 response, tempted by band below. *5 marks.*

Level	Marks	Evaluation	Explanation	Focus	Coherence	Specialist terminology
2	3–4	Relevant, not generic ✔	Well-explained	Focused	Mostly coherent	Used appropriately ✔
1	1–2	Outlined only	Limited ✔	Muddled	Muddled ✔	Absent or inappropriate
	0	No relevant content				

Comments Harlow's study is an appropriate evaluation but the first sentence is irrelevant. The description of findings is necessary to draw the conclusion. A reasonably explained point – between Level 1 and 2.

The second evaluation is briefer and lacks clarity. This pulls the mark into a Level 1 response. *2 marks.*

Understanding marking

AO1 + AO3 question: **Outline and evaluate the behavioural approach to treating phobias.** *(12 marks)*

Answer Phobias are a class of mental disorder associated with high levels of anxiety and avoidance of the phobic object. The behavioural approach to treating phobias is based on explaining phobias using the behavioural approach. Classical conditioning can be used to explain how they are acquired and the same thing can be used in their treatment. The method is called systematic desensitisation. This is based on the principles of conditioning, which is a behaviourist idea.

The steps involved are (1) Client taught to relax, (2) Create a hierarchy, (3) Start with least feared object and relax, (4) Work way to most feared. This can be done through flooding instead where the hierarchy is missed out and you just go straight to the most feared object. This has the difficulty of being quite traumatic and then the client may just give up, meaning that the therapy is not successful at all.

This has proved to be a good therapy and it makes sense because if people learn a phobia because of conditioning then it can be unlearned. Many people like this kind of therapy because you don't have to think about it. It's also good because you don't actually need a therapist to do it. If you read about it you could use it yourself to overcome a phobia.

On the negative side, as I have already said, some people may find it quite unpleasant and if they give up this means it won't be a very useful therapy. Behaviourist ideas are based on research with animals. In fact systematic desensitisation comes from experiments that were first done with cats, so the question is whether it really can be applied to humans. But often this is not true. An alternative might be to use drug therapies or CBT, both of which are effective ways to treat some mental disorders.

A real problem for systematic desensitisation is that it may just cure the symptoms. It could be that there was some deeper psychological cause of the disorder and this is not tackled using systematic desensitisation. All that is cured is the fear of an object rather than actual cause.

(364 words)

Level	Marks	Knowledge	Accuracy	Discussion	Focus	Clarity and organisation	Specialist terminology
4	10–12	Generally well-detailed	Accurate	Effective	Focused	Clear, coherent	Effective use
3	7–9	Evident	Occasional inaccuracies/ omissions ✔	Mostly effective ✔	Lacks focus ✔	Mostly clear and organised ✔	Mostly used effectively ✔
2	4–6	Limited ✔	Lacking in places	Limited effectiveness	Mainly descriptive	Lacking in places	Occasionally inappropriate
1	1–3	Very limited	Many inaccuracies	Limited or absent	Poor	Lacking clarity, poor organisation	Absent or inappropriate
0	0	No relevant content					

Examiner comments

Introduction contains little of merit, basic scene-setting in mentioning classical conditioning and identifying systematic desensitisation.

Very brief outline of an anxiety hierarchy which could be more clearly linked to phobias by using examples. Thus this is lacking detail.

The paragraph also contains a mention of flooding with a limitation.

A number of positive points strung together, only partly effective because there is not much explanation.

Seeing how questions are marked helps you see how to improve your own answers.

Repeat of previous point.

Second sentence onwards is a reasonably developed point, i.e. mostly effective.

Final paragraph is also mostly effective as the point is explained / elaborated.

Overall comments

Knowledge: limited, not detailed.

Accuracy: reasonable.

Evaluation: two points that are mostly effective and a number that are partly effective. Ratio of AO1 to AO3 is good.

Focus: lacks focus at the start.

Clarity and organisation: mostly clear but towards lower end of level.

Specialist terminology: mostly used appropriately but towards lower end of level.

Overall the level that best describes this answer is Level 3 but we are tempted lower, making this 7 marks (58%), probably Grade C (almost a B).

Conformity

Spec spotlight

Variables affecting conformity including group size, unanimity and task difficulty ~~as investigated by Asch.~~

Note that exam questions will focus on the variables that affect conformity not on Asch's procedure or baseline findings.

You must read any question carefully – only describe procedures if the question specifically asks for them.

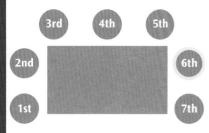

Baseline procedure

123 American male participants were tested individually, sitting last or next-to-last in a group of six to eight confederates.

They were shown two large cards. On one was a 'standard line'. On the other were three comparison lines. One of the three lines was the same length as the standard and the other two were always clearly different. Each group member stated which of the three lines matched the standard.

There were 18 'trials' involving different pairs of cards. On 12 of these ('critical trials') the confederates all gave the same clearly wrong answer.

Asch (1951) Baseline procedure

AIMS	Solomon Asch (1951) devised a procedure to measure the extent that people conformed to the opinion of others, even in a situation when the others' answers were clearly wrong.
	The baseline procedure is briefly described below left.

FINDINGS OF BASELINE STUDY	Asch found that the naïve participants conformed 36.8% of the time. This shows a high level of conformity when the situation is unambiguous.
	There were individual differences, 25% of the participants never gave a wrong answer (i.e. never conformed).
	75% conformed at least once.
	Asch conducted further studies where he showed that certain variables lead to less or more conformity. The details are given below.

Variables investigated by Asch

Variable 1 *Group size.*	Procedure – Asch varied the number of **confederates** in each group between 1 and 15 (total group size between 2 and 16).
	Findings – the relationship between group size and level of conformity was curvilinear.
	If there were two confederates, conformity to the wrong answer was 13.6%. When there were three confederates, conformity rose to 31.8%.
	Above three confederates, conformity rate levelled off. Adding more than three confederates made little difference.
	Explanation – people very sensitive to opinions of other people because just one confederate was enough to sway opinion.
Variable 2 *Unanimity.*	Procedure – Asch introduced a dissenting confederate – sometimes they gave the correct answer and sometimes a different wrong answer (but always disagreed with majority).
	Findings – in the presence of a dissenter, conformity reduced on average to less than a quarter of the level it was when the majority was unanimous.
	Conformity reduced if dissenter gave right or wrong answer.
	Explanation – having a dissenter enabled the naïve participant to behave more independently.
Variable 3 *Task difficulty.*	Procedure – Asch made the line-judging task harder by making stimulus line and comparison lines more similar in length.
	Thus it was difficult to see differences between the lines.
	Finding – conformity increased.
	Explanation – the situation is more ambiguous, so we are more likely to look to others for guidance and to assume they are right and we are wrong.
	This is informational social influence (see next spread) – it plays a greater role when the task becomes harder.

One limitation is that the situation and task were artificial.

Participants knew they were in a research study (demand characteristics). The task was trivial and there was no reason *not* to conform.

Also, Fiske (2014) argued 'Asch's groups were not very groupy' (not like real-life groups).

This means the findings do not **generalise** to everyday life (especially those situations where the consequences of conformity are important).

Another limitation is that Asch's findings have little application.

Only American men were tested by Asch. Neto (1995) suggested that women might be more conformist, possibly because they are more concerned about social relationships (and being accepted).

Also the US is an **individualist** culture and studies in **collectivist** cultures (e.g. China) have found higher conformity rates (Bond and Smith 1996). (See page 62 for note on individualist/collectivist.)

This means Asch's findings tell us little about conformity in women and people from some cultures.

One strength is other evidence to support Asch's findings.

Lucas *et al.* (2006) asked participants to solve 'easy' and 'hard' maths problems. Participants were given answers that (falsely) claimed to be from three other students.

The participants conformed more often (agreed with the wrong answers) when the problems were harder.

This shows Asch was correct that task difficulty is one variable affecting conformity.

Counterpoint

Conformity is more complex than Asch thought. Lucas *et al.*'s study showed that conformity was related to confidence (high confidence = less conformity).

This shows that individual-level factors interact with situational ones. But Asch did not investigate individual factors.

Evaluation extra: Asch's research raises ethical issues.

Asch's research increased our knowledge of why people conform, which may help avoid mindless destructive conformity.

But when participants are deceived they cannot give their **informed consent** to take part and may have a negative experience.

Therefore, we might still argue that the research was justified because there are a wide range of potential applications and the stress caused was minimal.

Apply it

Some friends are planning what they might do at the weekend. Most of them want to try out a new nightclub. But Sam fancies going to see a band he likes instead.

Briefly explain how each of the factors of group size, unanimity and task difficulty might influence whether or not Sam conforms to the majority.

Revision BOOSTER

When you evaluate Asch's research, don't be sidetracked into describing it first. It can be tempting to do this just to 'set the scene'. There is virtually no description of Asch's procedures or findings on this AO3 page. Follow this example, and stick to evaluation.

And they say social networking is killing the art of conversation.

Knowledge Check

1. Explain what Asch's research tells us about why people conform. **(4 marks)**

2. Referring to Asch's research, briefly explain how group size, unanimity and task difficulty affect conformity. **(2 marks + 2 marks + 2 marks)**

3. Evaluate Asch's research into conformity. **(6 marks)**

4. Outline **and** evaluate Asch's research. **(12 marks AS, 16 marks AL)**

Conformity: Types and explanations

Spec spotlight

Types of conformity: internalisation, identification and compliance.

Explanations for conformity: informational social influence and normative social influence.

Have you heard? Conformity is all about following the others.

Revision BOOSTER

Feel free to use examples as part of your AO1 description. It's an excellent way to demonstrate your knowledge and understanding of key concepts in conformity, such as internalisation, identification and compliance.

Two-process theory

Deutsch and Gerard (1955) brought ISI and NSI together in their two-process theory of social influence.

They argued that people conform because of two basic human needs: the need to be right (ISI) and the need to be liked (NSI).

Types of conformity

Internalisation. Think the group is right.	When a person genuinely accepts group norms. It results in a private as well as public change of opinions/behaviour.
	The change is usually permanent and persists in the absence of group members because attitudes have become part of how the person thinks (internalised).
Identification. Value the group.	When we identify with a group that we value, we want to become part of it.
	So we publicly change our opinions/behaviour, even if we don't privately agree with everything the group stands for.
Compliance. Temporary agreement.	Involves 'going along with others' in public, but privately not changing opinions/behaviour.
	This results in only a superficial change and the opinion/behaviour stops as soon as group pressure ceases.

Explanations for conformity

Informational social influence (ISI)

ISI is about information, a desire to be right.	Often we are uncertain about what behaviour or beliefs are right or wrong. You may not know the answer to a question in class, but if most of your class gives an answer, you go along with them because you feel they are probably right.
	ISI is a **cognitive** process – people generally want to be right. ISI leads to internalisation.
ISI occurs in situations that are ambiguous.	ISI is most likely in situations which are new or where there is some ambiguity, so it isn't clear what is right.
	It may happen when decisions have to be made quickly, when we assume the group is likely to be right.

Normative social influence (NSI)

NSI is about norms, a desire to behave like others and not look foolish.	NSI concerns what is 'normal' behaviour for a social group (i.e. norms). Norms regulate the behaviour of groups and individuals.
	NSI is an emotional rather than cognitive process – people prefer social approval rather than rejection. NSI leads to compliance.
NSI occurs in unfamiliar situations and with people you know.	NSI is most likely in situations where you don't know the norms and look to others about how to behave.
	NSI occurs in situations with strangers if you don't want to be rejected. Or with people we know because we are concerned about the social approval of friends.
	It may be more pronounced in stressful situations where people have a need for social support.

One strength of NSI is that there is research support.

Asch (1951) found many participants conformed rather than give the correct answer because they were afraid of disapproval.

When participants wrote down answers (no normative pressure), conformity fell to 12.5%.

This shows that at least some conformity is due to a desire not to be rejected by the group for disagreeing with them.

Another strength is research support for ISI.

Lucas et al. (2006) found participants conformed more to incorrect answers when maths problems were difficult (with easy problems, participants 'knew their own minds').

For hard problems the situation was ambiguous (unclear) so they relied on the answers they were given.

This supports ISI because the results are what ISI would predict.

Counterpoint

It is unclear if NSI or ISI operate in studies and real life. A dissenter may reduce the power of NSI (social support) or reduce the power of ISI (alternative source).

Therefore ISI and NSI are hard to separate and operate together in most real-world situations.

One limitation is individual differences in NSI.

Some people are concerned about being liked by others – nAffiliators who have a strong need for 'affiliation' (need to relate to other people).

McGhee and Teevan (1967) found that students who were nAffiliators were more likely to conform.

This shows NSI underlies conformity for some people more than for others – an individual difference not explained by a theory of situational pressures.

Evaluation extra: Is the NSI/ISI distinction useful?

Lucas et al.'s study shows that the NSI/ISI distinction may not be useful because it is impossible to work out which is operating (see counterpoint).

However, Asch's research supports both NSI (disapproval of a unanimous group strongly motivates conformity) and ISI (you assume the unanimous group knows better than you).

Therefore overall both concepts are useful because they can be identified and used to explain the reasons for conformity in studies and real-world situations.

Apply it

A man is lying on the pavement in a busy street. People are walking round him and ignoring him. No-one stops to see if there is anything wrong.

Miriam hated reading The Midwich Cuckoos *for her book group, but at the meeting said she loved it along with everyone else.*

1. Which of these scenarios shows ISI and which NSI? Give some reasons for your choice.

2. Can you think of any more examples?

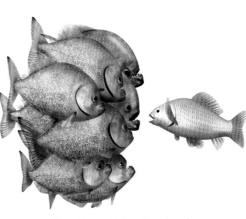

Sometimes it's tough swimming against the tide.

Knowledge Check

1. Give brief explanations of 'internalisation', 'identification' and 'compliance'.
   (2 marks + 2 marks + 2 marks)

2. Outline informational social influence **and** normative social influence as explanations of conformity.
   (6 marks)

3. Evaluate informational social influence **and** normative social influence as explanations of conformity.
   (6 marks)

4. Discuss what research has told us about why people conform.
   (12 marks AS, 16 marks AL)

Conformity to social roles

Spec spotlight

Conformity to social roles as investigated by Zimbardo.

Life was hard at the Premier Lodge, Prestatyn.

Revision BOOSTER

There are two major elements to describing Zimbardo's research – what he did (the procedure) and what he found (his findings). You can also include conclusions as part of what he found.

Be prepared – you may have to describe just the procedure, or just the findings, or possibly both.

Or you may be asked to discuss conformity to social roles and then just use the procedures/findings to support your understanding of the effects of social roles.

READ THE QUESTION CAREFULLY.

The Lucifer Effect

Zimbardo has in recent years developed his research to try and explain why good people can do evil things. He argues that evil behaviour is not the result of a few 'bad apples' contaminating the rest of the apples in the barrel. Instead, the barrel itself is rotten and it turns the apples in it rotten too. He calls this the Lucifer Effect and claims that it explains the behaviour of the guards in the SPE.

Chapter 1: Social influence

Zimbardo (1973) The Stanford prison experiment (SPE)

PROCEDURE

Zimbardo *et al.* (1973) set up a mock prison in the basement of the psychology department at Stanford University to investigate the effect of social roles on conformity.

21 male student volunteers were involved in the study – selected by psychological testing that showed them to be 'emotionally stable'.

They were **randomly allocated** to the role of guard or prisoner.

The social roles were encouraged by two routes:

1. Uniform

   Prisoners were strip-searched, given a uniform and number (no names), this encouraged de-individuation.

   Guards enforced rules, had own uniform with handcuffs, etc.

2. Instructions about behaviour

   Prisoners were told they could not leave but would have to ask for parole.

   Guards were told they had complete power over prisoners.

FINDINGS AND CONCLUSIONS

The guards played their roles enthusiastically and treated prisoners harshly.

The prisoners rebelled within two days – they ripped their uniforms, shouted and swore at the guards.

The guards retaliated with fire extinguishers and harassed the prisoners – reminder of their powerless role (e.g. frequent headcounts, including at night).

The guards' behaviour threatened the prisoners' psychological and physical health. For example:

1. After the rebellion was put down, the prisoners became subdued, anxious and depressed.

2. Three prisoners were released early because they showed signs of psychological disturbance.

3. One prisoner went on hunger strike; the guards attempted to force-feed him and punished him by putting him in 'the hole', a tiny dark closet.

The study was stopped after six days instead of the planned 14 days.

Social roles are powerful influences on behaviour – most conformed strongly to their role.

Guards became brutal, prisoners became submissive.

Other volunteers also easily conformed to their roles in the prison (e.g. the 'chaplain').

One strength of the SPE is the control over key variables.

Emotionally-stable participants were recruited and randomly allocated the roles of guard or prisoner.

The guards and prisoners had those roles only by chance. So their behaviour was due to the role itself and not their personalities.

This control increased the study's **internal validity**, so we have more confidence in drawing conclusions about the effect of social roles on conformity.

One limitation is that the SPE lacked the realism of a true prison.

Banuazizi and Mohavedi (1975) suggest participants were play-acting. Their performances reflected stereotypes of how prisoners and guards are supposed to behave.

One guard based his role on a character from the film *Cool Hand Luke*. Prisoners rioted because they thought that is what real prisoners did.

This suggests the SPE tells us little about conformity to social roles in actual prisons.

Counterpoint

Participants behaved as if the prison was real, e.g. 90% of conversations about prison life, Prisoner 416 believed it was a prison run by psychologists.

This suggests the SPE **replicated** the roles of guard and prisoner just as in a real prison, increasing internal validity.

Another limitation is that Zimbardo exaggerated the power of roles.

The power of social roles to influence behaviour may have been exaggerated in the SPE (Fromm 1973).

Only a third of the guards behaved brutally. Another third applied the rules fairly. The rest supported the prisoners, offering them cigarettes and reinstating privileges.

This suggests the SPE overstates the view that the guards were conforming to a brutal role and minimised dispositional influences (e.g personality).

Evaluation extra: Alternative explanation.

Zimbardo claimed participants naturally took on their social roles – just having a role meant that participants conformed to expectations associated with it.

However this doesn't explain those guards who were not brutal. Social identity theory (Reicher and Haslam 2006) argues only those who identify with the role of guard conform.

This shows that it is possible to resist situational pressures to conform to a social role, as long as the individual does not identify with that role.

Zimbardo's volunteers knew in advance if they were going to play the part of a prison inmate. Being arrested and strip-searched probably came as more of a surprise...

Knowledge Check

1. Outline the procedure **and** findings of **one** study into conformity to social roles.
   (6 marks)

2. Explain what research has shown about conformity to social roles. *(4 marks)*

3. Briefly discuss **two** limitations of Zimbardo's research.
   (6 marks)

4. Outline **and** evaluate research into conformity to social roles.
   (12 marks AS, 16 marks AL)

Obedience

Spec spotlight

Obedience, as investigated by Milgram.

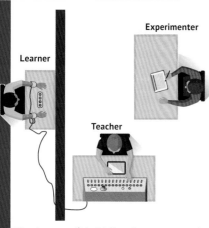

Learner

Experimenter

Teacher

The Learner ('Mr Wallace') was strapped into a chair in a separate room and wired with electrodes.

The Learner's task was to remember word pairs. The Teacher delivered shocks by pressing switches on a 'shock machine' labelled from 'slight shock' to 'danger – severe shock'.

If the Teacher felt unsure about continuing, the Experimenter used a sequence of four standard 'prods':

(Prod 1) 'Please continue' or 'Please go on.'

(Prod 2) 'The experiment requires that you continue.'

(Prod 3) 'It is absolutely essential that you continue.'

(Prod 4) 'You have no other choice, you must go on.'

Revision BOOSTER

Exam questions on Milgram's research rarely require any description of the procedure – yet students can't resist recording all the details. At most you need 100 words on procedural details – don't waste exam time doing more.

Focus on what the findings tell us about obedience.

Milgram (1963) Baseline obedience study

Stanley Milgram recruited 40 American male participants supposedly for a study of memory.

BASELINE PROCEDURE

Each participant arrived at Milgram's lab and drew lots for their role.

A **confederate** ('Mr Wallace') was always the 'Learner' while the true participant was the 'Teacher'.

An 'Experimenter' (another confederate) wore a lab coat.

The procedure is shown in the diagram (left) and described in the text below. The Teacher could hear but not see the Learner.

The Teacher had to give the Learner an increasingly severe electric 'shock' each time he made a mistake on a task. The shocks increased in 15-volt steps up to 450 volts.

The shocks were fake but the shock machine was labelled to make them look increasingly severe.

If the Teacher wished to stop, the Experimenter gave a verbal 'prod' to continue.

BASELINE FINDINGS

Key findings

12.5% (five participants) stopped at 300 volts.

65% continued to 450 volts (highest level).

Observations (qualitative data) – participants showed signs of extreme tension. Three had 'full-blown uncontrollable seizures'.

Other findings

Before the study Milgram asked 14 psychology students to predict how they thought the naïve participants would respond. The students estimated no more than 3% would continue to 450 volts (so the baseline findings were unexpected).

After the study, participants were debriefed. Follow-up questionnaire showed 84% were glad they had participated.

CONCLUSIONS

We obey legitimate authority even if that means that our behaviour causes harm to someone else.

Certain situational factors encourage obedience (Milgram investigated these, see next spread).

One strength is that replications have supported Milgram's research findings.

In a French TV documentary/game show, contestants were paid to give (fake) electric shocks when ordered by the presenter to other participants (actors) (Beauvois *et al.* 2012).

80% gave the maximum 460 volts to an apparently unconscious man. Their behaviour was like that of Milgram's participants, e.g. many signs of anxiety.

This supports Milgram's original findings about obedience to authority.

One limitation is that Milgram's study lacked internal validity.

Orne and Holland (1968) argued that participants guessed the electric shocks were fake. So they were 'play-acting'.

This was supported by Perry's discovery that only half of the participants believed the shocks were real (see top right).

This suggests that participants may have been responding to **demand characteristics**.

Counterpoint

However, Sheridan and King's (1972) participants gave real shocks to a puppy; 54% of males and 100% of females delivered what they thought was a fatal shock.

This suggests the obedience in Milgram's study might be genuine.

One limitation is that the findings are not due to blind obedience.

Haslam *et al.* (2014) found that every participant given the first three prods obeyed the Experimenter, but those given the fourth prod disobeyed.

According to social identity theory, the first three prods required identification with the science of the research but the fourth prod required blind obedience.

This shows that the findings are best explained in terms of identification with scientific aims and not as blind obedience to authority.

Evaluation extra: There are ethical issues.

The participants in this study were deceived e.g. they thought the shocks were real. Milgram dealt with this by debriefing participants.

Baumrind (1964) felt this deception could have serious consequences for participants and researchers e.g. no **informed consent** possible.

Therefore research can damage the reputations of psychologists and their research in the eyes of the public.

> Not everyone agrees with this conclusion. What do you think?

Perry's research

Perry (2013) analysed Milgram's archive of tape recordings. She made several discoveries that undermine the validity of Milgram's findings and conclusions, including:

- The 'Experimenter' frequently went 'off-script', for example he would vary the wording of the four prods and use them excessively (26 times with one unfortunate participant).

- Participants often voiced their suspicions about the shocks; Perry concluded that most of Milgram's participants realised that the shocks were fake.

Most people would look up to their boss as an example of an authority figure – though it obviously helps if your boss is thirteen feet tall.

Knowledge Check

1. Briefly describe the procedure used by Milgram to investigate obedience. *(4 marks)*
2. Explain what Milgram's research showed about obedience. *(4 marks)*
3. Explain **two** limitations of Milgram's research into obedience. *(6 marks)*
4. Outline **and** evaluate Milgram's research. *(12 marks AS, 16 marks AL)*

Obedience: Situational variables

Spec spotlight

Explanations for obedience: situational variables affecting obedience including proximity and location, as investigated by Milgram, and uniform.

Apply it

Think of a real-life situation (or more than one) in which proximity, location and uniform play a role in whether or not someone decides to obey an order.

Using evidence from Milgram's research, explain how each of these situational factors influences the decision to obey. Make sure your explanations are closely related to the situation(s).

Superman discovered that not all uniforms are equally authoritative.

Explanations for obedience based on situational variables

Proximity. Closeness of Teacher and Learner.	In the baseline study, the Teacher could hear the Learner but not see him.
	In the *proximity* variation, Teacher and Learner were in the same room and the obedience rate dropped from 65% to 40%.
	In the *touch proximity* variation, the Teacher forced the Learner's hand onto a shock plate. The obedience rate was 30%.
	In the *remote-instruction* variation, the Experimenter left the room and gave instructions by telephone. The obedience rate was 20.5% and participants often pretended to give shocks.
	Explanation – decreased proximity allows people to psychologically distance themselves from the consequences of their actions.
	For example, when the Teacher and Learner were physically separated, the Teacher was less aware of the harm done, so was obedient.
Location. Prestige of setting.	The study was conducted in a run-down building rather than at the prestigious Yale University (as in the baseline).
	Obedience dropped to 47.5%.
	Explanation – obedience was higher in the university because the setting was legitimate and had authority (obedience was expected).
Uniform. Communicates authority.	In the baseline study, the Experimenter wore a grey lab coat (a kind of uniform).
	In one variation, he was called away by an 'inconvenient' phone call at the start of the procedure. His role was taken over by an 'ordinary member of the public' in everyday clothes.
	Obedience fell to 20%, the lowest of these variations.
	Explanation – a uniform is a strong symbol of legitimate authority granted by society. Someone without a uniform has less right to expect obedience.

Graph showing all the variations.

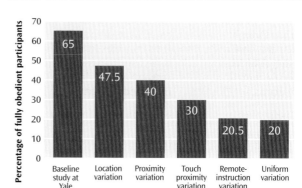

One strength is research support for the influence of situational variables.

Bickman's (1974) **confederates** dressed in different outfits (jacket/tie, milkman, security guard) and issued demands (e.g. pick up litter) to people on the streets of New York City.

People were twice as likely to obey the 'security guard' than the 'jacket/tie' confederate.

This shows that a situational variable, such as a uniform, does have a powerful effect on obedience.

Another strength is cross-cultural **replication** of Milgram's research.

Meeus and Raaijmakers (1986) worked with Dutch participants, who were ordered to say stressful comments to interviewees.

They found 90% obedience, and obedience fell when proximity decreased (person giving orders not present).

This shows that Milgram's findings are not limited to American males but are valid across cultures.

Counterpoint

However, Smith and Bond (1998) note that most replications took place in societies (e.g. Spain, Australia), culturally not that different from the US.

Therefore we cannot conclude that Milgram's findings about proximity, location and uniform apply to people in all (or most) cultures.

One limitation is low **internal validity** in the studies.

Orne and Holland (1968) suggested the variations (compared to baseline study) were even more likely to trigger suspicion because of the extra experimental manipulation.

In the variation where the Experimenter was replaced by 'a member of the public', even Milgram recognised this was so contrived that some participants may have worked it out.

Therefore it is unclear whether the results are due to obedience or because the participants saw the deception and 'play-acted' (i.e. were influenced by **demand characteristics**).

Evaluation extra: The danger of the situational perspective.

Milgram's conclusions suggest situational factors determine obedience.

Mandel (1998) argues this offers an excuse (alibi) for genocide. Situational explanations hugely oversimplify the causes of the Holocaust and are offensive to survivors.

This permits others to excuse destructive behaviour in terms of 'I was just obeying orders'.

Revision BOOSTER

An effective way of evaluating research is to offer counter-arguments.

For instance, imagine you have explained how Milgram's variations lack validity because of methodological issues. You can then go on to explain the 'other side of the coin'.

For example, manipulating one situational variable (e.g. proximity) at a time in lab conditions can be artificial, but it also allows us to see the effects of each variable on obedience more clearly.

'Look – if you're going to steal my party outfit idea, the least you can do is lose the hat...'

Knowledge Check

1. Milgram investigated the effects of situational variables on obedience. Briefly outline the findings of his research into any **two** of these variables. (6 marks)

2. Evaluate Milgram's research into the effects of situational variables on obedience. (6 marks)

3. Outline research into the effect of situational variables on obedience **and** discuss what this tells us about why people obey. (12 marks AS, 16 marks AL)

Obedience: Situational explanations

Spec spotlight

Explanations for obedience: agentic state and legitimacy of authority.

Being in an agentic state is like being a 'puppet' of authority – just ask those two.

Apply it

Think about a time when you did something you were told to do (by a parent, teacher, friend, police officer, etc.). Contrast this with an occasion when someone told you to do something and you refused.

Explain why you did or did not obey in terms of agentic state and legitimacy of authority.

Eichmann and the Holocaust

Milgram's initial interest in obedience was sparked by the trial of Adolf Eichmann in 1961 for war crimes. Eichmann had been in charge of the Nazi death camps and therefore had a pivotal role in the Holocaust. His defence at his trial was that the important decisions were taken by others in the hierarchy above him and that he was 'only obeying orders'.

Explanation 1: Agentic state

Agentic state. Act on behalf of another person.	Milgram proposed that obedience to destructive authority occurs because a person becomes an 'agent', someone who acts for or in place of another. In an agentic state a person feels no personal responsibility for their actions.
Autonomous state. Not an agent.	'Autonomy' means to be independent or free. So a person in an autonomous state behaves according to their principles and feels responsible for their actions.
Agentic shift. Moving to agentic state.	The shift from autonomy to being an 'agent' is called the agentic shift. Milgram suggested that this occurs when we perceive someone else as an authority figure. This person has power because of their position in a social hierarchy.
Binding factors. Reduce 'moral strain'.	Binding factors are aspects of a situation that allow the person to ignore or minimise the damaging effect of their behaviour and reduce the 'moral strain' they feel. Milgram proposed a number of strategies the individual uses, such as shifting the responsibility to the victim or denying the damage they are doing to victims.

Explanation 2: Legitimacy of authority

We obey people further up a social hierarchy.	Most societies are structured hierarchically. People in certain positions hold authority over the rest of us, e.g. parents, teachers, police officers, nightclub bouncers.
Authorities have legitimacy through society's agreement.	The power that authorities wield is legitimate because it is agreed by society. Most of us accept that authority figures should exercise social power over others to allow society to function smoothly.
We hand control over to authority figures.	People with legitimate authority have the power to punish others. We give up some independence to people we trust to exercise authority properly. We learn to accept authority during childhood (parents, teachers, etc.).
Leaders use legitimate powers for destructive purposes.	History has shown that some leaders (e.g. Hitler, Stalin, Pol Pot) use legitimate authority destructively, ordering people to behave in cruel and dangerous ways.

One strength is that the agentic state explanation has research support.

Most of Milgram's participants asked the 'Experimenter', 'Who is responsible if Mr Wallace (the Learner) is harmed?'

When the Experimenter replied 'I'm responsible' the participants went through the procedure quickly without objecting.

This shows participants acted more easily as an agent when they believed they were not responsible for their behaviour.

One limitation is the agentic shift doesn't explain many research findings.

For example, Rank and Jacobson (1977) found that most nurses disobeyed a doctor's order to give an excessive drug dose.

The doctor was an authority figure but the nurses remained autonomous and did not shift into an agentic state. The same is true for some of Milgram's participants.

This shows that agentic shift can only explain obedience in some situations.

Evaluation extra: Obedience alibi revisited.

The men of Battalion 101 did not have direct orders to shoot civilians in a Polish town (Mandel 1998).

Even so, they did perform the massacre, behaving autonomously.

This suggests that the agentic shift is not required for destructive behaviour.

One strength is legitimacy can explain cultural differences.

Research shows that countries differ in obedience to authority.

For example, 16% of Australian women obeyed (Kilham and Mann 1974), 85% of German participants did (Mantell 1971).

This shows that authority is more likely seen as legitimate in some cultures, reflecting upbringing.

One limitation is legitimacy cannot explain all (dis)obedience.

People may disobey even when they accept the legitimacy of the hierarchical authority structure.

For example, most of Rank and Jacobson's nurses were disobedient, as were some of Milgram's participants.

This suggests that innate tendencies towards (dis)obedience may be more important than legitimacy of authority.

Evaluation extra: Real-world crimes of obedience.

Research shows that some people disobey legitimate authority, e.g. Rank and Jacobson (above) – the nurses disobeyed a doctor even in a hierarchy.

But soldiers at My Lai obeyed their commanding officer, maybe he had more power to punish than a doctor (Kelman and Hamilton 1989).

Therefore there is some evidence in real-world situations that respect for legitimate authority can lead to destructive obedience.

'And as a punishment young man you can sit on this awful beige sofa for the rest of the day.'

Knowledge Check

1. Outline **one or more** explanations for obedience.
   (6 marks)
2. Outline what research has shown about the agentic state explanation for obedience.
   (4 marks)
3. Outline 'legitimacy of authority' as an explanation for obedience. *(4 marks)*
4. Discuss explanations for obedience. Refer to the agentic state **and** legitimacy of authority in your answer.
   (12 marks AS, 16 marks AL)

Obedience: Dispositional explanation

Spec spotlight

Dispositional explanation for obedience: the Authoritarian Personality.

People with authoritarian personalities get willingly trodden on by those above and are happy to tread on those below.

Dispositional versus situational

Adorno had the same aim as Milgram, to understand the Holocaust. But they came to very different conclusions. Milgram was convinced that everyone has the potential to behave in destructively obedient ways given the 'right' circumstances. This is a situational explanation of obedience. In contrast Adorno believed that the causes of obedience lie within the individual themselves, a dispositional view.

Apply it

Two students are discussing why some people are more obedient than others. Freda thinks that some people have an 'obedient' type of personality, which developed when they were children. Stefan thinks that we are all capable of being obedient if the situation is right.

What arguments could Freda use to support her view?

The Authoritarian Personality

High obedience is pathological.	Adorno *et al.* (1950) believed that unquestioning obedience is a psychological disorder, and tried to find its causes in the individual's personality.
Extreme respect for authority and contempt for 'inferiors'.	Adorno *et al.* concluded that people with an Authoritarian Personality are especially obedient to authority. They: • Have exaggerated respect for authority and submissiveness to it. • Express contempt for people of inferior social status. Authoritarians tend to follow orders and view 'other' groups as responsible for society's ills.
Originates in childhood (e.g. overly strict parenting).	Authoritarian Personality forms in childhood through harsh parenting – extremely strict discipline, expectation of absolute loyalty, impossibly high standards, and severe criticism. It is also characterised by conditional love – parents' love depends entirely on how their child behaves.
Hostility is displaced onto social inferiors.	These experiences create resentment and hostility in the child, but they cannot express these feelings directly against their parents because they fear reprisals. So the feelings are displaced onto others who are weaker – this is scapegoating. This is a **psychodynamic** explanation.

Adorno *et al.* (1950) The Authoritarian Personality

	The study investigated unconscious attitudes towards other ethnic groups of more than 2000 middle-class white Americans.
PROCEDURE	Several scales were developed, including the potential-for-fascism scale (F-scale). Examples from the F-scale (rated on scale 1 to 6 where 6 = agree strongly): • 'Obedience and respect for authority are the most important virtues for children to learn.' • 'There is hardly anything lower than a person who does not feel great love, gratitude and respect for his parents.'
FINDINGS	Authoritarians (who scored high on the F-scale and other measures) identified with 'strong' people and were contemptuous of the 'weak'. They were conscious of their own and others' status, showing excessive respect and deference to those of higher status.
	Authoritarian people also had a **cognitive** style where there was no 'fuzziness' between categories of people, with fixed and distinctive stereotypes (prejudices) about other groups.

One strength is evidence that authoritarians are obedient.

Elms and Milgram (1966) interviewed 20 fully obedient participants from Milgram's original obedience studies.	They scored significantly higher on the F-scale than a comparison group of 20 disobedient participants.	This suggests that obedient people may share many of the characteristics of people with an Authoritarian Personality.

Counterpoint

However, subscales of the F-scale showed that obedient participants had characteristics that were unusual for authoritarians. For example they did not experience high levels of punishment in childhood.

This suggests a complex link and means that authoritarianism is not a useful predictor of obedience.

One limitation is authoritarianism can't explain a whole country's behaviour.

Millions of individuals in Germany displayed obedient and anti-Semitic behaviour – but can't all have had the same personality.	It seems unlikely the majority of Germany's population had an Authoritarian Personality. A more likely explanation is that Germans identified with the Nazi state.	Therefore *social identity theory* (see right) may be a better explanation.

One limitation is that the F-scale is politically biased.

Christie and Jahoda (1954) suggest the F-scale aims to measure tendency towards extreme right-wing ideology.	But right-wing and left-wing authoritarianism (e.g. Chinese Maoism) both insist on complete obedience to political authority.	Therefore Adorno's theory is not a comprehensive dispositional explanation as it doesn't explain obedience to left-wing authoritarianism, i.e. it is politically biased.

Evaluation extra: Flawed evidence.

The F-scale has been used in many research studies that have led to an explanation of obedience based on the Authoritarian Personality.	However, the F-scale is flawed (Greenstein), e.g. people who tend to agree to the statements (response bias) are scored as authoritarian.	Therefore, explanations of obedience based on research with the F-scale may not be valid.

Revision BOOSTER

One way of evaluating the Authoritarian Personality is to contrast it with a situational explanation (i.e. Milgram's research). But do this effectively: don't just describe Adorno's research and then Milgram's research and leave it at that. Compare them: you could highlight how Milgram's research better explains the evidence.

Greenstein said the F-scale was a 'comedy of methodological errors'. Shakespeare would have understood.

Social identity theory

This is the view that our behaviour and attitudes are strongly influenced by those of the groups we identify with (our ingroups).

Knowledge Check

1. Explain what is meant by 'Authoritarian Personality' in relation to obedience. *(2 marks)*
2. Describe **one** dispositional explanation for obedience. *(6 marks)*
3. Evaluate the Authoritarian Personality explanation for obedience. *(6 marks)*
4. Describe **and** evaluate the Authoritarian Personality as an explanation for obedience. *(12 marks AS, 16 marks AL)*

Resistance to social influence

Spec spotlight

Explanations of resistance to social influence, including social support and locus of control.

Resistance: to refuse to accept or be influenced by something – oh yes, Snowy knew all about that.

Revision BOOSTER

Some exam questions are accompanied by a 'stem', or invented scenario. They give you the chance to demonstrate your knowledge and understanding of psychology by using it to explain something.

So it's really important that you refer to the stem, not just once but throughout your answer. Don't just make passing references – use quotes from the stem, tease out specific content in the stem that you can explain with your knowledge.

Apply it

It's Saturday afternoon and Sid is deep into his revision for an exam on Monday. Three friends call round to persuade him to drop everything for an evening of 'fun and games'. Sid is tempted, but knows his exam is important.

1. Explain, in terms of Sid's locus of control (internal or external), whether or not he would go along with his friends.

2. Explain how social support could help him to resist his friends' influence.

Explanation 1: Social support

Resisting conformity. Dissenting peer.	Pressure to conform is reduced if other people are not conforming.
	Asch's research showed that the dissenter doesn't have to give the 'right' answer.
	Simply someone else not following the majority frees others to follow their own conscience. The dissenter acts as a 'model'.
	The dissenter shows the majority is no longer unanimous.
Resisting obedience. Obedience is reduced by one other dissenting partner.	Pressure to obey can be reduced if another person is seen to disobey.
	Milgram's research – obedient behaviour greatly decreased in the *disobedient peer* condition (from 65% to 10%).
	The participant may not follow the disobedient peer but the dissenter's disobedience frees the participant to act from their own conscience.
	A disobedient model challenges the legitimacy of the authority figure.

Explanation 2: Locus of control (LOC)

Internals place control with themselves. *Externals* place control outside themselves.	Rotter (1966) described internal versus external LOC.
	Internals believe things that happen to them are largely controlled by themselves (e.g. doing well or badly in an exam depends on how hard you work).
	Externals believe things happen outside their control. If they fail an exam they say it was because they had a bad teacher or had bad luck because the questions were hard.
There is a continuum.	LOC is not just being internal or external – there is a scale from one to the other and people differ in their position on it.
	High internals at one end and high externals at the other, low internals and low externals lie in-between.
Internals show greater resistance to social influence.	People with internal LOC are more likely to resist pressures to conform or obey.
	(1) If someone takes personal responsibility for their actions (good or bad) they are more likely to base their decisions on their own beliefs.
	(2) People with high internal LOC are more confident, more achievement-oriented and have higher intelligence – traits that lead to greater resistance (also traits of leaders, who have less need for social approval).

One strength is evidence for the role of support in resisting conformity.

In a programme to help pregnant adolescents to resist pressure to smoke, social support was given by an older 'buddy' (Albrecht *et al.* 2006).

These adolescents were less likely to smoke at the end of the programme than a **control group** who did not have a buddy.

This shows social support can help young people resist social influence in real-world situations.

Another strength is evidence for the role of support for dissenting peers.

Gamson *et al.*'s (1982) groups asked to give evidence for an oil company to use in a smear campaign.

29 out of 33 groups (88%) rebelled against orders, much higher than in Milgram's studies.

This shows how supporters can undermine legitimacy of authority and reduce obedience.

Simon was getting the impression that his 'quiet afternoon in' with the kids wasn't quite going to plan.

Evaluation extra: Social support explanation.

Only 3% of Allen and Levine's (1971) participants resisted conformity when there was no supporter. But 64% resisted when a dissenter refused to conform.

However, only 36% resisted when the supporter clearly had poor eyesight and could not be relied on to judge the lines.

This shows the explanation is valid because we would expect *less* resistance when participants believed social support was *not* helpful.

One strength is evidence to support the role of LOC in resisting obedience.

Holland (1967) repeated the Milgram study and measured whether participants were internals or externals.

37% of internals did not continue to the highest shock level (they showed greater resistance). Only 23% of externals did not continue.

Therefore resistance partly related to LOC, increasing the **validity** of this explanation of disobedience.

One limitation is not all research supports the role of LOC in resistance.

Twenge *et al.* (2004) analysed data from American locus of control studies over 40 years (1960 to 2002), showing that people have become more independent but also more external.

This is surprising – if resistance was linked to internal LOC we would expect people to have become more internal.

Therefore LOC may not be a valid explanation of resistance to social influence.

Evaluation extra: Limited role of LOC.

A lot of studies (e.g. Holland 1967) show that having an internal LOC is linked with being able to resist social influence.

However, Rotter (1982) pointed out that LOC only significantly influences behaviour in new situations. In familiar situations, our previous responses are always more important.

Therefore, the validity of the LOC explanation is limited because it can predict resistance in some situations but not in others.

Revision BOOSTER

Quality is always more important than quantity – but many students don't believe this.

Students generally prefer to give a list of lots of different evaluations instead of explaining just one or two evaluations in detail.

It is more difficult to provide one detailed evaluation – which is why that gains more credit than a list-like answer.

Knowledge Check

1. Outline how social support can help people to resist social influence. *(4 marks)*

2. Briefly describe the locus of control explanation of resistance to social influence. *(4 marks)*

3. Briefly explain **one** limitation of locus of control as an explanation of resistance to social influence. *(2 marks)*

4. Outline **and** evaluate **two** explanations of resistance to social influence. *(12 marks AS, 16 marks AL)*

Minority influence

Spec spotlight

Minority influence including reference to consistency, commitment and flexibility.

Critics have suggested that getting people to persuade others that blue is green is not really something that would happen in everyday life. Having said that, I'm sure we've all met someone who would argue black is white, just for the sheer hell of it.

Moscovici *et al.'s* (1969) study

Procedure

A group of six people (four participants, two **confederates**) viewed 36 blue-coloured slides of varying intensities. They were asked to state whether the slides were blue or green.

In one condition, both confederates consistently said the slides were green.

In another condition, the confederates were inconsistent (green 24 times, blue 12 times).

The procedure was repeated with a **control group** (no confederates).

Findings

Consistent minority: participants gave the same wrong answer (green) on 8.42% of trials.

Inconsistent minority: agreement fell to 1.25%.

Control group: wrongly identified colour just 0.25% of the time.

Minority influence

Minority influence.	Refers to how one person or small group influences the beliefs and behaviour of other people.
	The minority may influence just one person, or a group of people (the majority) – this is different from conformity where the majority does the influencing. (Conformity is sometimes referred to as 'majority influence'.)
Internalisation. Beliefs changed.	Minority influence leads to internalisation – both public behaviour and private beliefs are changed.
	Three processes – consistency, commitment, flexibility.
Consistency. Always doing the same thing.	Means the minority's view gains more interest.
	Consistency makes others rethink their own views ('Maybe they've got a point if they all think this way and they have kept saying it').
	• *Synchronic consistency* – people in the minority are all saying the same thing.
	• *Diachronic consistency* – they've been saying the same thing for some time.
Commitment. Showing deep involvement.	Helps gain attention e.g. through extreme activities.
	Activities must create some risk to the minority to demonstrate commitment to the cause.
	Augmentation principle – majority pay even more attention ('Wow, he must really believe in what he's saying, so perhaps I ought to consider his view').
Flexibility. Showing willingness to listen to others.	The minority should balance consistency and flexibility so they don't appear rigid.
	Nemeth (1986) argued that being consistent and repeating the same arguments and behaviours is seen as rigid and off-putting to the majority.
	Instead, the minority should adapt their point of view and accept reasonable counterarguments.
Explaining the process of minority influence.	Individuals think deeply about the minority position because it is new/unfamiliar.
	Snowball effect – over time, more people become 'converted' (like a snowball gathering more snow as it rolls along). There is a switch from the minority to the majority.
	The more this happens, the faster the rate of conversion.
	Gradually the minority view becomes the majority and social change has occurred.

One strength is research supporting consistency.

Moscovici et al. (1969, see facing page) found a consistent minority opinion had a greater effect on other people than an inconsistent opinion.

Wood et al. (1994) conducted a **meta-analysis** of almost 100 similar studies and found that minorities seen as being consistent were most influential.

This confirms that consistency is a major factor in minority influence.

Although the other gummy bears would tease him because of his tiny paws and oversized head, Barrington knew that if he could just get one of them on side, the rest would surely follow.

Another strength is research showing role of deeper processing.

Martin et al. (2003) gave participants a message supporting a particular viewpoint, and measured attitudes. Then they heard an endorsement of view from either a minority or a majority. Finally heard a conflicting view, attitudes measured again.

Participants were less willing to change their opinions to the new conflicting view if they had listened to a minority group than if they listened to a majority group.

This suggests that the minority message had been more deeply processed and had a more enduring effect.

Apply it

A campaigner against obesity argues that the main culprit is sugar. His solution is to cut out from our diet all cakes, biscuits, sweets, chocolate and fizzy drinks. Not surprisingly, as most people enjoy these foods, they are not keen to accept the message.

Explain three ways in which the campaigner might be able to persuade the majority to change their view.

Counterpoint

In research studies (e.g. Martin et al.) majority/minority groups distinguished in terms of numbers. But there is more to majorities/minorities than just numbers (e.g. power, status, commitment).

This means research studies are limited in what they tell us about real-world minority influence.

One limitation is minority influence research often involves artificial tasks.

Moscovici et al.'s task was identifying the colour of a slide, far removed from how minorities try to change majority opinion in the real world.

In jury decision-making and political campaigning, outcomes are vastly more important, maybe a matter of life or death.

Findings of studies lack **external validity** and are limited in what they tell us about how minority influence works in real-world situations.

Revision BOOSTER

At least six concepts related to minority influence are outlined on this spread. A really good description will include most of them (range) and in some detail (depth).

However, in an extended writing answer with evaluation you must carefully limit the amount of AO1 to give yourself plenty of time for evaluation. It is good to consider what you would include in 150 words of AO1 (about right for 6 marks).

Evaluation extra: Power of minority influence.

Agreement with the minority was only 8% in Moscovici et al.'s study – minority influence must be quite rare, so perhaps not a useful concept.

However, more participants agreed with the minority when writing their answers privately. So those who do 'go public' must be the 'tip of the iceberg' and hold their new views strongly (internalisation).

Therefore minority influence is valid – it is a relatively unusual form of social influence but can change people's views powerfully and permanently (conversion).

Knowledge Check

1. Explain what is meant by 'minority influence'. *(2 marks)*
2. Outline research (theories and/or studies) into minority influence. *(6 marks)*
3. Explain the importance of consistency, commitment **and** flexibility in minority influence. *(6 marks)*
4. Outline **and** evaluate research into minority influence. *(12 marks AS, 16 marks AL)*

Spec spotlight

The role of social influence processes in social change.

The snowball effect – a great thing when it leads to positive social change. When it leads to an avalanche – not so good.

Apply it

A psychology teacher is explaining to her students how times have changed: 'There was a time when a lot of people thought homosexuality was wrong. It was even considered by psychology and psychiatry to be a mental disorder. But these days most people in Britain are much more accepting and are in favour of gay marriage.'

Referring to the teacher's comment, explain how social influence processes can lead to social change.

Examples of social change

The example of social change used here is the movement for African-American civil rights in the 1950s and 60s. But there are many other cases of change where social influence has been crucial, such as: the spread of environmentalism (e.g. recycling), the eradication of apartheid in South Africa, the collapse of Communism in Eastern Europe, the campaign for women's votes (the Suffragette movement), the growth of the Internet...

Lessons from minority influence research

(1) Drawing attention.	Segregation in 1950s America – places such as certain schools and restaurants in the southern states were exclusive to whites. Civil rights marches *drew attention* to the situation by providing *social proof* of the problem.
(2) Consistency.	People took part in the marches on a large scale. Even though it was a minority of the American population, they displayed *consistency* of message and intent.
(3) Deeper processing.	This activism meant that many people who had accepted the status quo began thinking *deeply* about the unjustness of it.
(4) *Augmentation principle.*	'Freedom riders' were both white as well as black people who boarded buses in the south to challenge separate seating for black people. Many were beaten. The personal risk strengthened (augmented) their message.
(5) *Snowball effect.*	Civil rights activists (e.g. Martin Luther King) gradually got the attention of the US government. In 1964 the Civil Rights Act was passed. Change happens bit by bit just as a rolling snowball grows as it gathers more snow.
(6) *Social cryptomnesia.*	Social change came about but some people have no memory (*cryptomnesia*) of the events leading to that change.

Lessons from conformity research

Dissenters make social change more likely.	Asch's research – variation where one **confederate** always gave correct answers. This broke the power of the majority encouraging others to dissent. This demonstrates potential for social change.
Normative social influence (NSI).	Environmental and health campaigns exploit conformity by appealing to NSI. They provide information about what others are doing, e.g. reducing litter by printing normative messages on bins ('Bin it – others do').

Lessons from obedience research

Disobedient models make change more likely.	Milgram's research: disobedient models in the variation where a confederate refused to give shocks. The rate of obedience in genuine participants plummeted.
Gradual commitment leads to 'drift'.	Zimbardo (2007) – once a small instruction is obeyed, it becomes more difficult to resist a bigger one. People 'drift' into a new kind of behaviour.

One strength is support for normative influence in social change.

Nolan *et al.* (2008) hung messages on front doors of houses. The key message was most residents are trying to reduce energy usage.

Significant decreases in energy use compared to **control group** who saw messages to save energy with no reference to other people's behaviour.

This shows conformity can lead to social change through the operation of NSI.

Counterpoint

Exposing people to social norms does not always change their behaviour. Foxcroft *et al.* (2015) reviewed 70 studies of programmes using social norms to reduce alcohol intake. There was only a small effect on drinking quantity and no effect on drinking frequency.

This shows that NSI does not always produce long-term social change.

Another strength is that minority influence explains social change.

Nemeth (2009) says that minority arguments cause people to engage in divergent thinking (broad, active information search, more options).

This thinking leads to better decisions and creative solutions to social problems.

This shows that minorities are valuable because they stimulate new ideas and open people's minds.

Another limitation is deeper processing may apply to majority influence.

Mackie (1987) disagrees with the view that minority influence causes individuals in the majority to think deeply about an issue.

Majority influence creates deeper processing because we believe others think as we do. When a majority thinks differently, this creates pressure to think about their views.

Therefore a central element of minority influence has been challenged, casting doubt on its **validity** as an explanation of social change.

Do you agree with this conclusion?

Evaluation extra: Barriers to social change.

The steps involved in the process of social change provide practical advice for minorities wanting to influence a majority (e.g. be consistent).

Even so, majorities still often resist change because they find the minority unappealing ('tree-huggers'). But even this can be counteracted (Bashir *et al.* 2013).

This shows that minority influence research does provide practical applications that eventually influence majorities to change.

Revision BOOSTER

When writing about social change, avoid turning your answer into one about minority influence. You can do this by including other forms of social influence, such as conformity and obedience.

But be very careful to link these processes with the central issue – social change itself. Use a specific example, either your own or one given to you in a stem/scenario.

Sometimes it just takes one to get the ball rolling...

...and the rest will follow.

Knowledge Check

1. Briefly explain what is meant by 'social change'. *(2 marks)*
2. Using an example, outline the role of social influence processes in bringing about social change. *(6 marks)*
3. Evaluate the role of social influence in social change. *(6 marks)*
4. Outline **and** evaluate research into the role of social influence processes in social change. *(12 marks AS, 16 marks AL)*

Coding, capacity and duration of memory

Spec spotlight

Short-term memory and long-term memory. Features of each store: coding, capacity and duration.

STM = short-term memory

LTM = long-term memory

Long-term memories are those memories that are enduring – the ones that are with you for a long time.

Revision BOOSTER

When you learn about any study it is useful to distinguish the procedures (P) from the findings/conclusions (F).

Some exam questions ask you to write about what a researcher did (= P).

Some questions ask you to write about what a researcher did and what they found (= P and F).

You may use a study as evaluation, then only the findings/conclusions are creditworthy.

The good thing about having a bad memory is that jokes can be funny more than once...

Coding – Baddeley (1966) Acoustic and semantic

PROCEDURE

Acoustically similar words (e.g. cat, cab, can) or dissimilar (e.g. pit, few, cow).

Semantically similar (e.g. great, large, big) or dissimilar (e.g. good, huge, hot).

FINDINGS

Immediate recall worse with acoustically similar words, STM is acoustic.

Recall after 20 minutes worse with semantically similar words, LTM is semantic.

Capacity – Jacobs (1887) Testing digit span

PROCEDURE

Researcher reads four digits and increases until the participant cannot recall the order correctly. Final number = digit span.

FINDINGS

On average, participants could repeat back 9.3 numbers and 7.3 letters in the correct order immediately after they were presented.

Capacity – Miller (1956) Magic number 7 ± 2

PROCEDURE

Miller observed everyday practice, noted that things come in sevens – notes of musical scale, days of the week, deadly sins, etc.

FINDINGS

The span of STM is about 7 items (plus or minus 2) but is increased by chunking – grouping sets of digits/letters into meaningful units.

Duration STM – Peterson and Peterson (1959) Consonant syllables

PROCEDURE

24 students were given a consonant syllable (e.g. YCG) to recall and a 3-digit number to count backwards from. The retention interval was varied: 3, 6, 9, 12, 15 or 18 seconds.

FINDINGS

After 3 seconds – average recall was about 80%. After 18 seconds it was about 3%. STM duration without rehearsal is up to 18 seconds.

Duration LTM – Bahrick *et al.* (1975) Yearbook photos

PROCEDURE

Participants were 392 Americans aged between 17 and 74.

1. Recognition test – 50 photos from high school yearbooks.
2. Free recall test – Participants listed names of their graduating class.

FINDINGS

Recognition test – 90% accurate after 15 years, 70% after 48 years.

Free recall test – 60% recall after 15 years, 30% after 48 years.

One strength of Baddeley's study is that it identified two memory stores.

Later research showed that there are exceptions to Baddeley's findings.

But STM is mostly acoustic and LTM is mostly semantic.

This led to the development of the **multi-store model** (next spread).

One limitation of Baddeley's study is that it used artificial stimuli.

The words used had no personal meaning to the participants so tells us little about coding for everyday memory tasks.

When processing more meaningful information, people use semantic coding even for STM.

This means the findings of this study have limited application.

My short-term memory is really bad...and also my short-term memory is really bad.

One strength of Jacobs' study is that it has been replicated.

This is an old study and may have lacked adequate controls (**confounding variables** e.g. participants being distracted).

Despite this, Jacobs' findings have been confirmed in later controlled studies (e.g. Bopp and Verhaeghen 2005).

This shows that Jacobs' study is a valid measure of STM digit span.

One limitation of Miller's research is it may overestimate STM capacity.

For example, Cowan (2001) reviewed other research.

He concluded that the capacity of STM was only about 4 (plus or minus 1) chunks.

This suggests that the lower end of Miller's estimate (5 items) is more appropriate than 7 items.

One limitation of Peterson and Peterson's study is the meaningless stimuli.

We sometimes try to recall meaningless things so the study is not completely irrelevant.

But recall of consonant syllables does not reflect meaningful everyday memory tasks.

Therefore the study lacked **external validity**.

One strength of Bahrick et al.'s study is it had high external validity.

Everyday meaningful memories (e.g. of people's faces and names) were studied.

When lab studies were done with meaningless pictures to be remembered, recall rates were lower (e.g. Shepard 1967).

This means that Bahrick et al.'s findings reflect a more 'real' estimate of the duration of LTM.

Apply it

Nadiya was using a pedestrian crossing when a car came speeding past her, almost knocking her down. She managed to get the car's registration – PF54 VXR – but had nothing to write it down with.

1. How long does Nadiya have before she forgets the car's registration (duration)?
2. Does she have enough room in her STM to remember it (capacity)?
3. What form will her memory of it take (coding)?

Knowledge Check

1. Explain **two** differences between short-term and long-term memory. *(2 marks + 2 marks)*
2. Explain how psychologists have investigated the duration of short-term memory. *(4 marks)*
3. Explain what research has shown about the duration of short-term memory. *(2 marks)*
4. Identify **and** explain the types of coding used in short- **and** long-term memory. *(4 marks)*
5. Describe **and** evaluate research into coding, capacity **and** duration of **either** short-term memory **or** long-term memory. *(12 marks AS, 16 marks AL)*

The multi-store model of memory

Spec spotlight

The multi-store model of memory: sensory register, short-term memory and long-term memory. Features of each store: coding, capacity and duration.

On the right is the multi-store model of memory. Above is a multi-storey car park. They sound a bit similar. That's pretty much all they have in common. So not that helpful really. Sorry.

Revision BOOSTER

If you have to describe/outline the MSM, there are two aspects you should include:

· The structure of the model.

· The processes involved.

Structure refers basically to the memory stores, sensory register, STM and LTM. Outline these one at a time. And remember that material from the previous spread is relevant, so you can describe the coding, capacity and duration of these stores.

Process refers to what happens to information as it flows through the memory system. Describe this step-by-step from start to finish: how information gets into memory, how it is passed from store to store (role of rehearsal), and how it is recalled (retrieval from LTM).

Atkinson and Shiffrin (1968) Multi-store model (MSM)

Separate memory stores.	The MSM describes how information flows through the memory system. Memory is made of three stores linked by processing.

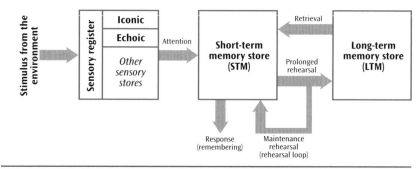

Sensory register (SR).	All stimuli from the environment (e.g. the sound of someone talking) pass into the SR. This part of memory is not one store but five, one for each sense. • Coding – modality-specific, depends on the sense (visual in iconic, acoustic in echoic, etc.). • Duration – very brief, less than half a second (see research on facing page). • Capacity – very high, e.g. over one hundred million cells in one eye, each storing data.
Transfer from SR to STM.	Information passes further into memory only if attention is paid to it (attention is the key process).
Short-term memory (STM).	A limited capacity store of temporary duration. • Coding – acoustic (based on sound). • Duration – about 18 seconds unless the information is rehearsed. • Capacity – between 5 and 9 (7 ± 2) items before some forgetting occurs (Cowan argues for around 5).
Transfer from STM to LTM.	Maintenance rehearsal occurs when we repeat (rehearse) material to ourselves. We can keep information in STM as long as we rehearse it. If we rehearse it long enough, it passes into LTM.
Long-term memory (LTM).	A permanent memory store. • Coding – mostly semantic (i.e. in terms of meaning). • Duration – potentially up to a lifetime. • Capacity – potentially unlimited.
Retrieval from LTM.	When we want to recall information stored in LTM it has to be transferred back to STM by a process called *retrieval*.

One strength is research support showing STM and LTM are different.

Baddeley (1966) found that we tend to mix up words that sound similar when using our STMs (so STM coding is acoustic).

But we mix up words that have similar meanings when we use our LTMs (which shows LTM coding is semantic).

This supports the MSM's view that these two memory stores are separate and independent.

Counterpoint

Despite such apparent support, the studies tend not to use everyday information (e.g. faces, names). They use digits/letters (Jacobs) or meaningless consonant syllables (Peterson and Peterson).

Therefore the MSM may not be a valid model of how memory works in everyday life where memory tends to involve meaningful information.

One limitation is evidence suggesting there is more than one STM store.

KF had amnesia (Shallice and Warrington 1970), STM recall for digits was poor when he heard them, but much better when he read them.

Other studies confirm there may also be a separate STM store for non-verbal sounds (e.g. noises).

Therefore the MSM is wrong to claim there is just one STM store processing different types of information.

Another limitation is prolonged rehearsal is not needed for STM–LTM transfer.

Craik and Watkins (1973) argued there are two types of rehearsal called maintenance and elaborative. Maintenance (amount of rehearsal) is the one described in the MSM.

But **elaborative rehearsal** is needed for long-term storage. This occurs e.g. when you link information to your existing knowledge, or think about its meaning.

This suggests that the MSM does not fully explain how long-term storage is achieved.

Do you agree with this conclusion?

Evaluation extra: Bygone model.

The MSM was a useful model that explained a lot of evidence at the time (e.g. differences between STM and LTM).

However, it has became clear that the MSM cannot account for many research findings (e.g. amnesia) and oversimplifies the nature of STM, LTM and rehearsal.

Therefore, the MSM was a good starting point for developing more valid models of memory that explain the research evidence better.

Apply it

A friend of yours is into acting, and is taking the lead role in Hamlet in a couple of months' time. He needs to learn a lot of lines and be able to remember them long-term.

Using your knowledge of the multi-store model, what advice might you give your friend about how best to remember his lines?

Duration of the iconic sensory register

Sperling (1960) tested the iconic SR (memory store). Participants saw a grid of digits and letters (below) for 50 milliseconds. They were either asked to write down all 12 items or they were told they would hear a tone immediately after the exposure and they should just write down the row indicated (top, middle, bottom). When asked to report the whole thing their recall was poorer (five items recalled, about 42%) than when asked to give one row only (three items recalled, 75%). This shows that information decays rapidly in the iconic sensory register.

Stimulus material used by Sperling.

7	1	V	F
X	L	5	3
B	4	W	7

Knowledge Check

1. According to the multi-store model of memory, explain what is meant by the 'sensory register'. **(2 marks)**

2. Outline the multi-store model of memory. **(6 marks)**

3. The multi-store model of memory has been heavily criticised. Outline **two** limitations of this model. **(3 marks + 3 marks)**

4. Describe **and** evaluate the multi-store model of memory. **(12 marks AS, 16 marks AL)**

Types of long-term memory

Spec spotlight

Types of long-term memory:
episodic, semantic, procedural.

'Memories...like the corners of my mind.'
Great song. Except the mind is a
metaphysical hypothetical construct
and doesn't have corners. Just saying.

Apply it

Amber is in year five at primary
school and has a spelling test every
Friday morning. Simon posts on
Facebook to describe how he asked
his girlfriend to marry him the night
before. Finn is in his second karate
class where everyone is practising the
moves they learned last week.

Identify **and** explain which types of
long-term memory are being used in
these situations.

Revision BOOSTER

You may need to explain a *difference*
between two types of LTM (see
Knowledge Check). A common
mistake when doing this is to
describe one type of LTM, then a
second type, without a connection
between the two. You must identify
an actual difference.

A good way of doing this is to choose
a feature of memory that one type
of LTM has but another type does
not. For example, we might say: 'One
difference between episodic and
semantic memories is the extent to
which we are taught them – no one
teaches you your episodic memories
but many semantic ones are taught'.

LTM store 1: Episodic memory

Stores events (episodes) from our lives.	This store has been likened to a diary of daily personal experiences (episodes).
	For example, your most recent visit to the dentist, the psychology class you had yesterday, the breakfast you ate this morning.
Episodic memories are complex.	They are time-stamped – you remember when they happened and how they relate in time.
	They involve several elements – people, places, objects and behaviours are woven into one memory.
	You have to make a conscious effort to recall them.

LTM store 2: Semantic memory

Stores our knowledge of the world.	Semantic memory is like a combination of an encyclopaedia and a dictionary.
	For example, it includes knowledge of such things as how to apply to university, the taste of an orange, and the meaning of words.
Semantic memories are not time-stamped.	They are not time-stamped, e.g. we don't remember when we first heard about *Frozen*.
	They are less personal than episodic memories and more about facts/knowledge we all share.

LTM store 3: Procedural memory

Stores memories for actions and skills.	These are memories of how we do things.
	For example, driving a car or playing table tennis.
Recall occurs without awareness or effort.	These skills/actions become automatic with practice.
	Explaining the step-by-step procedure (e.g. changing gear) is hard because you do it without conscious recall.

One strength is case study evidence of different types of LTM.

Clinical studies of amnesia (HM and Clive Wearing) showed both had difficulty recalling events that had happened to them in their pasts (episodic memory).

But their semantic memories were relatively unaffected (e.g. HM did not need the concept of 'dog' explained to him). Procedural memories were also intact (e.g. Clive Wearing still played the piano).

This supports the view that there are different memory stores in LTM because one store can be damaged but other stores are unaffected.

Counterpoint

Researchers lack control in clinical case studies – they do not know anything about the person's memory before brain damage.

Therefore clinical studies are limited in what they can tell us about different types of LTM.

One limitation is conflicting findings about types of LTM and brain areas.

Buckner and Petersen (1996) reviewed research findings and concluded that semantic memory is located in the left **prefrontal cortex** and episodic with the right prefrontal cortex.

But other studies (e.g. Tulving *et al.* 1994) have found that semantic memory was associated with the *right* prefrontal cortex and the reverse for episodic memory.

This challenges any neurophysiological evidence to support types of memory as there is poor agreement on where each type might be located.

Another strength is helping people with memory problems.

Memory loss in old age is specific to episodic memory – it is harder to recall memories of recent experiences although past episodic memories are intact.

Belleville *et al.* (2006) devised an intervention for older people targeting episodic memory, which improved their memory compared to a **control group**.

This shows that distinguishing between types of LTM enables specific treatments to be developed.

Evaluation extra: Same or different?

More recently Tulving (2002) has said episodic memory is a 'specialised subcategory' of semantic – an intact semantic memory can function with a damaged episodic but not vice versa.

However Hodges and Patterson (2007) found that some patients with Alzheimer's disease can form new episodic memories but not semantic ones.

Therefore episodic and semantic memories are closely related but ultimately different forms of LTM.

Ah, the birth of your first child.

What a moment that is. It still seems like it was yesterday.

When they handed me this tiny, precious thing – smiling, beautiful, everything in perfect miniature.

I can still remember the feeling of bewildered awe …

… because I'd ordered a pizza.

Revision BOOSTER

On the left we have identified THREE evaluation points (plus an evaluation extra), and for each provided THREE levels of elaboration.

On page 6 we suggested there are two routes for doing evaluation in an AS essay (6 marks AO3) – either do TWO well-elaborated points or THREE 'intermediate' evaluations.

Knowledge Check

1. Explain what is meant by 'episodic memory'. *(2 marks)*

2. There are three types of long-term memory. Choose any **two** and explain **one** difference between them. *(2 marks)*

3. Using an example, describe **one** type of long-term memory. *(3 marks)*

4. Briefly outline semantic memory as a type of long-term memory. *(2 marks)*

5. Outline **and** evaluate types of long-term memory. *(12 marks AS, 16 marks AL)*

The working memory model

Spec spotlight

The working memory model: central executive, phonological loop, visuo-spatial sketchpad and episodic buffer. Features of the model: coding and capacity.

You need to know about coding and capacity for each store in the WMM.

CE: coding is flexible; capacity is very limited. (NB Recent views suggest there may be no storage capacity at all.)

PL: coding is acoustic, capacity is about two seconds' worth of what you can say.

VSS: coding is visual and spatial, capacity is three or four objects.

EB: coding is flexible, capacity is about four 'chunks'.

Revision BOOSTER

The topic of memory can help you to revise more effectively. Consider using *mnemonics*, a method of improving memory. Try making up a sentence using the letters (in order) of the WMM: CE, PL, VSS, EB. Include one or two rude words because these are especially memorable. Here's a clean attempt: Certain Events Produce Long Very Silly Sausages Every Birthday.

The key phrases in the first column of the table on the right are meant to be triggers to help you remember the main content – see page 7 for an explanation of effective revision.

Baddeley and Hitch (1974) Working memory model (WMM)

WMM is a model of STM.

The WMM is concerned with the 'mental space' that is active when, for example, working on an arithmetic problem or playing chess or comprehending language, etc.

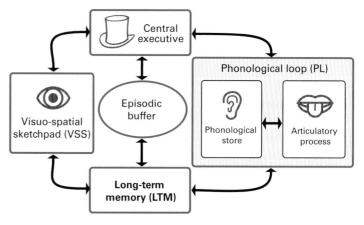

Central executive (CE) allocates subsystems.	Supervisory role – monitors incoming data, directs attention and allocates subsystems to tasks. It has a very limited storage capacity.
Phonological loop (PL) consists of a phonological store and an articulatory process.	PL deals with auditory information and preserves the order in which the information arrives. It is subdivided into: • Phonological store: stores the words you hear. • Articulatory process: allows maintenance rehearsal (repeating sounds to keep them in WM while they are needed).
Visuo-spatial sketchpad (VSS).	Stores visual and/or spatial information when required, (e.g. recalling how many windows your house has). Logie (1995) subdivided the VSS into: • Visual cache: stores visual data. • Inner scribe: records arrangement of objects in visual field.
Episodic buffer (EB), temporary storage.	Added in 2000. It is a temporary store for information. Integrates visual, spatial, and verbal information from other stores. Maintains sense of time sequencing – recording events (episodes) that are happening. Links to LTM.

One strength of the model is support from clinical evidence.

For example, Shallice and Warrington (1970) studied patient KF who had a brain injury.

His STM for auditory information was poor (damaged PL) but he could process visual information normally (intact VSS).

This supports the WMM view that there are separate visual and acoustic memory stores.

Counterpoint

KF may have had other impairments which explained poor memory performance, apart from damage to his PL.

This challenges evidence from clinical studies of brain injury.

Another strength is that dual task performance studies support the VSS.

Baddeley et al.'s (1975) participants found it harder to carry out two visual tasks at the same time than do a verbal and a visual task together. (Same for two verbal tasks.)

This is because both visual tasks compete for the same subsystem (VSS). There is no competition with a verbal and visual task.

Therefore there must be a separate subsystem that processes visual input (VSS) and also a separate system for verbal processes (PL).

One limitation is a lack of clarity over the central executive.

Baddley (2003) said the CE was the most important but the least understood component of working memory.

There must be more to the CE than just being 'attention' e.g. it is made up of separate subcomponents.

Therefore the CE is an unsatisfactory component and this challenges the integrity of the model.

Evaluation extra: Validity of the model.

Dual-task studies support the WMM because they show that there must be separate components processing visual (VSS) and verbal information (PL).

However, these studies are highly-controlled and use tasks that are unlike everyday working memory tasks (e.g. recalling random sequences of letters).

This challenges the **validity** of the model because it is not certain that working memory operates this way in everyday situations.

Apply it

You are walking down the street. A car driver is lost so pulls over to ask you for directions to a petrol station. Fortunately, you know where one is, so you think for a moment and then describe the route the driver should take.

Explain what is happening in your working memory as you perform this task. Refer to all four components of the working memory store in your explanation.

I don't have an issue with multitasking – I can do several things equally badly at the same time.

Download suggested answers to the Knowledge Check questions from tinyurl.com/y8kjyvwe

Knowledge Check

1. In relation to the working memory model, explain what is meant by the 'phonological loop' **and** 'episodic buffer'.
   (2 marks + 2 marks)

2. Outline the working memory model. *(6 marks)*

3. Outline **one** strength **and one** limitation of the working memory model.
   (2 marks + 2 marks)

4. Describe **and** evaluate the working memory model.
   (12 marks AS, 16 marks AL)

Explanations for forgetting: Interference

Spec spotlight

Explanations for forgetting: proactive and retroactive interference.

Interference is all about mental confusion between similar tasks – which is why you should never do the ironing when you're expecting a phone call. Ouch!

Revision BOOSTER

Always remember that there are two major aspects of any research study – what the researchers did (the procedure) and what they found (the findings).

Where do conclusions fit in? You can include these as part of the findings.

Graph showing findings from McGeoch and McDonald's study.

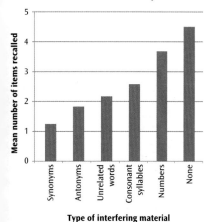

Interference theory

Interference: when two pieces of information disrupt each other.	Forgetting occurs in LTM because we can't get access to memories even though they are available.
Proactive interference (PI) – old interferes with new.	PI occurs when an older memory disrupts a newer one. For example, a teacher learns many names in the past and can't remember names of her current class.
Retroactive interference (RI) – new interferes with old.	RI happens when a newer memory disrupts an older one. For example, a teacher learns many new names this year and can't remember the names of her previous students.
Interference is worse when memories are similar.	This may be because: • In PI previously stored information makes new information more difficult to store. • In RI new information overwrites previous memories which are similar.

McGeoch and McDonald (1931) Effects of similarity

PROCEDURE

Participants were asked to learn a list of words to 100% accuracy (i.e. could recall them perfectly).

Then they were given a new list to learn. The new material varied in the degree to which it was similar to the old:

• Group 1: synonyms – words had same meanings as the originals.
• Group 2: antonyms – words had opposite meanings to the originals.
• Group 3: unrelated – words unrelated to the original ones.
• Group 4: consonant syllables.
• Group 5: three-digit numbers.
• Group 6: no new list – participants just rested (**control condition**).

FINDINGS AND CONCLUSIONS

Performance depended on the nature of the second list. The most similar material (synonyms) produced the worst recall.

This shows that interference is strongest when the memories are similar. The findings are shown in the graph on the left.

One strength is some support for interference in real-world situations.

Baddeley and Hitch (1977) asked rugby players to recall the names of teams they had played against during a rugby season.

Players did not play the same number of games (injuries). Those who played most (more interference) had poorest recall.

This shows that interference operates in some everyday situations, increasing the **validity** of the theory.

Counterpoint

Interference in everyday situations is unusual because the necessary conditions are relatively rare e.g. similarity of memories/learning does not occur often.

Therefore most everyday forgetting may be better explained by other theories (e.g. retrieval failure due to lack of cues).

One limitation is that interference effects may be overcome using cues.

Tulving and Psotka (1971) gave participants lists of words organised into categories (not told what they were).

Recall of first list was 70% but fell with each new list (proactive interference). When given a cued recall test (names of categories) recall rose again to 70%.

This shows that interference causes just a temporary loss of access to material still in LTM – not predicted by theory.

Another strength is support from drug studies.

Material learned just before taking *diazepam* recalled better than a placebo group one week later – this is *retrograde facilitation* (Coenen and van Luijtelaar 1997).

The drug stopped new information reaching brain areas that process memories, so it could not retroactively interfere with stored information (Wixted).

This shows that the forgetting is due to interference – reducing the interference reduced the forgetting.

Not everyone agrees with this conclusion. What do you think?

Evaluation extra: Validity issues.

Lab studies of interference have tight control of **confounding variables** (e.g. time), thus clear link between interference and forgetting.

However, most research is unlike everyday forgetting. In everyday life we often learn something and recall it much later (e.g. revising for exams).

This means that because research is mostly lab-based it may overestimate the importance of interference as a cause of forgetting.

Jen's anger at being called by his previous girlfriend's name was not dispelled by John cheerfully pointing out that he had just experienced 'proactive interference'.

Explanations for forgetting: Retrieval failure

Spec spotlight

Explanations for forgetting: retrieval failure due to absence of cues.

Every pool player's nightmare – an absence of cues.

Revision BOOSTER

Retrieval failure theory can help you revise. Meaningful cues can really help you learn and remember because they act as 'triggers'. That's why key terms are useful – to lead you into recall of related material. Headings, subheadings and sub-subheadings (the more the merrier) are also helpful cues, because they mean you organise your material so it is easier to learn and recall.

Even the image below could itself be a cue to the details of Godden and Baddeley's study.

Retrieval failure due to the absence of cues

Lack of cues can cause retrieval failure.	When information is initially placed in memory, associated cues are stored at the same time. If the cues are not available at the time of retrieval, you might not access memories that are actually there.
Encoding specificity principle (Tulving 1983).	Cues help retrieval if the same ones are present both (1) at encoding (when we learn the material) and (2) at retrieval (when we are recalling it). If the cues available at encoding and retrieval are different (or if cues are entirely absent) there will be some forgetting.
Links between encoded cues and material to-be-remembered.	Meaningful links – the cue 'STM' leads you to recall lots of material about short-term memory. Not meaningful links: • Context-dependent forgetting – recall depends on external cue (e.g. weather or a place). • State-dependent forgetting – recall depends on internal cue (e.g. feeling upset, being drunk).

Godden and Baddeley (1975) Context-dependent forgetting

PROCEDURE	Deep-sea divers learned word lists and were later asked to recall them: • Condition 1: Learn on land – recall on land. • Condition 2: Learn on land – recall underwater. • Condition 3: Learn underwater – recall on land. • Condition 4: Learn underwater – recall underwater.
FINDINGS AND CONCLUSIONS	Accurate recall was 40% lower in conditions 2 and 3 (mismatched contexts) than in conditions 1 and 4 (matched contexts). Retrieval failure was due to absence of encoded context cues at time of recall – material was not accessible (i.e. forgotten).

Carter and Cassaday (1998) State-dependent forgetting

PROCEDURE	Participants learned lists of words/prose and later recalled them. • Condition 1: Learn when on drug – recall on drug. • Condition 2: Learn when on drug – recall not on drug. • Condition 3: Learn when not on drug – recall on drug. • Condition 4: Learn when not on drug – recall not on drug.
FINDINGS AND CONCLUSIONS	Recall was significantly worse in conditions 2 and 3 (mismatched cues) compared with conditions 1 and 3 (matched cues). When the cues at encoding are absent at retrieval (e.g. you are drowsy when recalling material but had been alert when you learned it) then there is more forgetting.

One strength is that retrieval cues have real-world application.

People often go to another room to get an item but forget what they wanted, but they remember again when they go back to the original room.

When we have trouble remembering something, it is probably worth making the effort to recall the environment in which you learned it first.

This shows how research can remind us of strategies we use in the real world to improve our recall.

Another strength is the impressive range of supporting evidence.

For example, Godden and Baddeley (divers) and Carter and Cassaday (drugs) show that lack of cues at recall leads to everyday forgetting.

In fact, Eysenck and Keane (2010) argue that retrieval failure is perhaps the main reason for forgetting in LTM.

This evidence shows that retrieval failure due to lack of cues occurs in everyday life as well as in highly-controlled labs.

Counterpoint

Baddeley (1997) argues that different contexts have to be very different indeed before an effect is seen (e.g. on land versus underwater). Learning something in one room and recalling it in another is unlikely to result in much forgetting because the environments are not different enough.

This means that retrieval failure due to lack of contextual cues may not explain much everyday forgetting.

One limitation is that context effects vary in recall and recognition.

Godden and Baddeley (1980) **replicated** their underwater experiment using a recognition test instead of recall.

There was no context-dependent effect. Findings were the same in all four conditions whether the contexts for learning and recall matched or not.

This suggests that retrieval failure is a limited explanation for forgetting because it only applies when a person has to recall information rather than recognise it.

Evaluation extra: Problems with the ESP.

Retrieval failure theory is supported by research showing that forgetting occurs when there is a mismatch (or absence) of cues – the encoding specificity principle (ESP).

However, we cannot independently establish whether a cue has really been encoded or not – so the argument for the role of cues is circular.

Therefore, the ESP is not scientifically testable, so we cannot be certain that forgetting is due to retrieval failure.

Apply it

Saeed is a university student who is planning to become a teacher. So he does some work experience at his old primary school, a place he hasn't been anywhere near in almost ten years. But as soon as Saeed steps through the doors, long-forgotten memories of primary school days come flooding back to him.

1. Explain why this happened to Saeed.

2. What does his experience tell us about 'forgetting'?

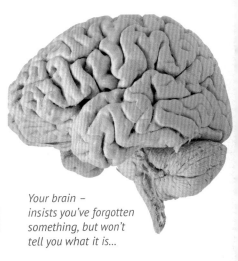

Your brain – insists you've forgotten something, but won't tell you what it is...

Knowledge Check

1. In relation to forgetting, explain what is meant by an 'absence of cues'. *(2 marks)*

2. Outline retrieval failure as an explanation for forgetting. *(4 marks)*

3. The retrieval failure explanation for forgetting has been criticised. Outline **two** limitations of this explanation. *(2 marks + 2 marks)*

4. Outline **and** evaluate retrieval failure as an explanation for forgetting. *(12 marks AS, 16 marks AL)*

Eyewitness testimony: Misleading information

Spec spotlight

Factors affecting the accuracy of eyewitness testimony, misleading information, including leading questions and post-event discussion.

A leading question is one that suggests a certain answer because of the way it is phrased. For example, 'Was the knife in his left hand?' implies that is where the knife was.

In post-event discussion (PED), witnesses to an event discuss what they have experienced. This could affect the accuracy of their recall.

Apply it

A bank has been robbed by a group of three gunmen in broad daylight. There are at least 15 witnesses to this crime so the police now have a lot of interviewing to do. However, one officer is worried because many of the witnesses know each other and have been discussing the crime.

Explain why the police officer is right to be concerned.

Loftus and Palmer (1974) Leading questions

PROCEDURE	45 participants (students) watched film clips of car accidents and then answered questions about speed. Critical question: 'About how fast were the cars going when they hit each other?'
	Five groups of participants, each given a different verb in the critical question: hit, contacted, bumped, collided or smashed.
FINDINGS	The verb 'contacted' produced a mean estimated speed of 31.8 mph. For the verb 'smashed', the mean was 40.5 mph.
	The *leading question* (verb) biased eyewitness recall of an event. The verb 'smashed' suggested a faster speed of the car than 'contacted'.

Why do leading questions affect EWT?

Response-bias explanation.	Wording of a question has no enduring effect on an eyewitness's memory of an event, but influences the kind of answer given.
Substitution explanation.	Wording of a question does affect eyewitness memory, it interferes with the original memory, distorting its accuracy.

Gabbert *et al.* (2003) Post-event discussion

PROCEDURE	Paired participants watched a video of the same crime, but filmed so each participant could see elements in the event that the other could not.
	Both participants discussed what they had seen on the video before individually completing a test of recall.
FINDINGS	71% of participants wrongly recalled aspects of the event they did not see in the video but had heard in the discussion. **Control group** – there was no discussion and no subsequent errors.
	This was evidence of memory conformity.

Why does post-event information affect EWT?

Memory contamination.	When co-witnesses discuss a crime, they mix (mis)information from other witnesses with their own memories.
Memory conformity.	Witnesses go along with each other to win social approval or because they believe the other witnesses are right.

One strength is real-world applications in the criminal justice system.

The consequences of inaccurate EWT are serious. Loftus (1975) argues police officers should be careful in phrasing questions to witnesses because of distorting effects.

Psychologists are sometimes expert witnesses in trials and explain limits of EWT to juries.

Therefore psychologists can improve how the legal system works and protect the innocent from faulty convictions based on unreliable EWT.

Counterpoint

Loftus and Palmer showed film clips – a different experience from a real event (less stress). Participants are also less concerned about the effect of their responses in a lab study (Foster *et al.* 1994).

Therefore researchers may be too pessimistic about the effects of misleading information – EWT may be more reliable than studies suggest.

One limitation of the substitution explanation is evidence challenging it.

Sutherland and Hayne (2001) found their participants recalled central details of an event better than peripheral ones, even when asked misleading questions.

This is presumably because their attention was focused on the central features and these memories were relatively resistant to misleading information.

Therefore the original memory of the event survived and was not distorted, which is not predicted by the substitution explanation.

Another limitation is that evidence does not support memory conformity.

Skagerberg and Wright's (2008) participants discussed film clips they had seen (in one version the mugger had dark brown hair and the other light brown).

The participants recalled a 'blend' of what they had seen and what they had heard from their co-witness, rather than one or the other (e.g. said hair was 'medium brown').

This suggests that the memory itself is distorted through contamination by post-event discussion and is not the result of memory conformity.

Evaluation extra: Demand characteristics.

Lab studies give researchers high control over variables (high **internal validity**), so they can demonstrate that misleading post-event information causes inaccurate EWT.

But lab experiments suffer from **demand characteristics** – participants want to help so they guess when they can't answer a question (low internal validity).

Therefore to maximise internal validity researchers should reduce demand characteristics by removing the cues that participants use to work out the hypothesis.

Revision BOOSTER

Don't confuse evaluation and description. Students often think they are doing well on evaluation and are disappointed to find they haven't got high marks. But this is usually because they aren't evaluating at all – they're just describing. For example, you might evaluate misleading information by pointing to the supporting evidence. But if all you do is say what the evidence is (e.g. what Loftus and Palmer found), that's description.

'So would you like the useless 1-year guarantee or the fantastic 5-year guarantee?'

Knowledge Check

1. Explain what is meant by 'eyewitness testimony'.
   (2 marks)

2. Explain what is meant by 'misleading information' in relation to eyewitness testimony. *(2 marks)*

3. Outline **two** factors that may affect the accuracy of eyewitness testimony.
   (2 marks + 2 marks)

4. Outline research into post-event discussion as a factor affecting the accuracy of eyewitness testimony. *(4 marks)*

5. Discuss what research has told us about the effect of misleading information on the accuracy of eyewitness testimony.
   (12 marks AS, 16 marks AL)

Eyewitness testimony: Anxiety

Spec spotlight

Factors affecting the accuracy of eyewitness testimony: anxiety.

Weapon focus

When a crime involves a weapon, this creates anxiety. A witness's attention is then focused on the weapon, leaving less attention for other details of the event.

Revision BOOSTER

Yerkes-Dodson can help you with exams – when it comes to performance, a little bit of anxiety is OK. So you shouldn't worry if exams (or even just the thought of them) make you a bit anxious.

But too much anxiety can be crippling, and might prevent you doing some revision or performing at your best on the day. If this applies to you, it's probably a good idea to learn how to reduce anxiety.

One word of advice though – being on top of your revision can be a very good antidote to anxiety.

Yerkes-Dodson Law

The inverted-U theory states that performance will increase with stress, but only to a certain point, where it decreases drastically.

Johnson and Scott (1976) Anxiety has a negative effect

PROCEDURE

Participants sat in a waiting room believing they were going to take part in a lab study.

- *Low-anxiety condition* – participants heard a casual conversation and then saw a man walk through the waiting room carrying a pen with grease on his hands.
- *High-anxiety condition* – a heated argument was accompanied by the sound of breaking glass. A man then walked through the room holding a knife covered in blood (creates anxiety and 'weapon focus').

Participants were later asked to pick the man from a set of 50 photographs.

FINDINGS AND CONCLUSIONS

49% of participants in the low-anxiety condition and 33% of high-anxiety participants were able to identify the man.

The *tunnel theory of memory* argues that people have enhanced memory for central events. Weapon focus as a result of anxiety can have this effect.

Yuille and Cutshall (1986) Anxiety has a positive effect

PROCEDURE

In an actual crime a gun-shop owner shot a thief dead. There were 21 witnesses, 13 agreed to participate in the study.

Participants were interviewed 4–5 months after the incident. The information recalled was compared to the police interviews at the time of the shooting.

Witnesses rated how stressed they felt at the time of the incident.

FINDINGS AND CONCLUSIONS

Witnesses were very accurate in what they recalled and there was little change after 5 months. Some details were less accurate, e.g. age/weight/height.

Participants who reported the highest levels of stress were most accurate (about 88% compared to 75% for the less-stressed group).

Anxiety does not appear to reduce the accuracy of EWT for a real-world event and may even enhance it.

Explaining the contradictory findings

Inverted-U theory.	Yerkes and Dodson (1908) argue that the relationship between performance and arousal/stress is an inverted U, as in the diagram on the left.
Affects memory.	Deffenbacher (1983) reviewed 21 studies of EWT with contradictory findings on the effects of anxiety on recall. He suggested the Yerkes-Dodson effect could explain this – both low and high levels of anxiety produce poor recall whereas optimum levels can lead to very good recall.

One limitation is that anxiety may not be relevant to weapon focus.

Johnson and Scott's participants may have focused on the weapon not because they were anxious but because they were surprised.

Pickel (1998) found accuracy in identifying the 'criminal' was poorest when the object in their hand was unexpected e.g. raw chicken and a gun in a hairdressers (both unusual).

This suggests the weapons effect is due to unusualness rather than anxiety/threat and so tells us nothing about the specific effects of anxiety on recall.

One strength is supporting evidence for negative effects.

Valentine and Mesout (2009) used heart rate (objective measure) to divide visitors to the London Dungeon's Labyrinth into low- and high-anxiety groups.

High-anxiety participants were less accurate than low-anxiety in describing and identifying a target person.

This supports the claim that anxiety has a negative effect on immediate eyewitness recall of a stressful event.

Another strength is supporting evidence for positive effects.

Christianson and Hübinette (1993) interviewed actual witnesses to bank robberies – some were direct victims (high anxiety) and others were bystanders (less anxiety).

They found more than 75% accurate recall across all witnesses. Direct victims (most anxious) were even more accurate.

This suggests that anxiety does not affect the accuracy of eyewitness recall and may even enhance it.

Counterpoint

Christianson and Hübinette interviewed witnesses long after the event. Many things happened that the researchers could not control (e.g. post-event discussions).

Therefore lack of control over **confounding variables** may be responsible for the (in)accuracy of recall, not anxiety.

Evaluation extra: Problems with inverted-U theory.

The inverted-U theory appears to be a reasonable explanation of the contradictory findings linking anxiety with both increased and decreased eyewitness recall.

However, it only focuses on physical anxiety and ignores other elements, including cognitive (how we think about a stressful event affects what we recall).

Therefore the inverted-U explanation is probably too simplistic to be useful e.g. anxious thoughts may not always lead to symptoms of anxiety but may block memory.

Knowledge Check

1. Explain what is meant by 'anxiety' in the context of eyewitness testimony. *(2 marks)*
2. Outline how anxiety may be a factor affecting the accuracy of eyewitness testimony. *(4 marks)*
3. Describe **and** evaluate anxiety as a factor affecting the accuracy of eyewitness testimony. *(12 marks AS, 16 marks AL)*

Spec spotlight

Improving the accuracy of eyewitness testimony, including the use of the cognitive interview.

A witness had described the suspect as being 'a bit on the green side'. It seemed that the police finally had their man.

Apply it

Imagine you are a police officer working in a police force that routinely uses the cognitive interview. You are interviewing a witness to a stabbing in which the victim survived but with serious injuries.

1. For each of the four main techniques of the CI, write a question that you could ask the witness.

2. Explain **three** ways in which you could use the enhanced CI in this situation.

The cognitive interview (CI)	
Based on psychological understanding of memory.	Fisher and Geiselman (1992) claimed that EWT could be improved if the police use techniques based on psychological insights into how memory works.
	They called it the cognitive interview to indicate its foundation in **cognitive** psychology.
	Rapport (understanding) is established with interviewee using four main techniques.
1. Report everything.	Witnesses are encouraged to include every detail of an event, even if it seems irrelevant or the witness is not confident about it.
	Seemingly trivial details could be important and may trigger other memories.
2. Reinstate the context.	The witness returns to the original crime scene 'in their mind' and imagines the environment (e.g. the weather, what they could see) and their emotions (e.g. what they felt).
	This is based on the concept of *context-dependent forgetting* (see page 40). Cues from the context may trigger recall.
3. Reverse the order.	Events are recalled in a different order (e.g. from the end back to the beginning, or from the middle to the beginning).
	This prevents people basing their descriptions on their expectations of how the event must have happened rather than the actual events.
	It also prevents dishonesty (harder to produce an untruthful account if it has to be reversed).
4. Change perspective.	Witnesses recall the incident from other people's perspectives. How would it have appeared to another witness or to the perpetrator?
	This prevents the influence of expectations and *schema* on recall. Schema are packages of information developed through experience. They generate a framework for interpreting incoming information.
Plus the *Enhanced cognitive interview* (ECI).	Fisher *et al.* (1987) developed additional elements of the CI.
	This includes a focus on the social dynamics of the interaction (e.g. knowing when to establish and relinquish eye contact).
	The enhanced CI also includes ideas such as reducing the eyewitness's anxiety, minimising distractions, getting the witness to speak slowly and asking open-ended questions.

One strength is research support for the effectiveness of the CI.

A **meta-analysis** by Köhnken *et al.* (1999) combined data from 55 studies comparing CI (and ECI) with the standard police interview.

The CI produced an average of 41% more correct information than the standard interview. Only four studies showed no difference.

This shows that the CI is effective in helping witnesses recall information that is available but not accessible.

Counterpoint

Köhnken *et al.* also found increases in the amount of *in*accurate information, especially in the ECI (quantity over quality).

Therefore police officers need to be very careful about how they treat eyewitness evidence from CIs/ECIs.

One limitation is that some elements of the CI are more useful than others.

Milne and Bull (2002) found that each individual technique of the CI alone produced more information than the standard police interview.

But they also found that combining *report everything* and *reinstate the context* produced better recall than any other technique individually or combined.

This casts doubt on the credibility of the overall CI because some of the techniques are less effective than the others.

Another limitation of the CI is that it is time-consuming.

Police are reluctant to use the CI because it takes more time than the standard police interview (e.g. to establish rapport and allow the witness to relax).

The CI also requires special training but many forces do not have the resources to provide more than a few hours' training (Kebbell and Wagstaff 1997).

This suggests that the complete CI is not realistic for police officers to use and it might be better (as suggested above) to focus on just a few key elements.

Evaluation extra: Variations of the CI.

Police forces take a 'pick and mix' approach in practice which makes it hard to compare effectiveness in studies.

However, this approach makes the CI more flexible because police forces (or individuals) evolve their own approaches depending on what they think works best.

This variation is a benefit of the CI because it can be adapted to different situations, increasing its credibility for officers, though not for empirical research.

Revision BOOSTER

You might need to consider the use of a cognitive interview in an application exam question. Think about how, for example, a police officer would ask questions (remember the four techniques) and how this would affect responses from witnesses. Always consider the effects of questioning techniques on characters in any scenario.

'I'm sorry,' blurted out the woman desperately as she broke down. *'I just don't think I can learn any more about memory.'*

'OK,' replied her psychology teacher, *'let's move on to attachment then.'*

Knowledge Check

1. Explain what is meant by the 'cognitive interview'. *(2 marks)*
2. Describe the use of the cognitive interview to improve the accuracy of eyewitness testimony. *(6 marks)*
3. The cognitive interview uses four main techniques to improve the accuracy of eyewitness testimony. Briefly outline any **two** of these techniques. *(4 marks)*
4. Discuss the cognitive interview as a method of improving the accuracy of eyewitness testimony. *(12 marks AS, 16 marks AL)*

Caregiver–infant interactions

Spec spotlight

Caregiver–infant interactions in humans: reciprocity and interactional synchrony.

What is attachment?

An attachment is a close two-way emotional bond between two individuals in which each sees the other as essential for their own emotional security. We can recognise an attachment when people display the following behaviours:

- *Proximity* (staying physically close to the attachment figure).
- *Separation distress* (being upset when an attachment figure leaves).
- *Secure-base behaviour* (babies leaving the attachment figure but regularly returning to them when playing).

Apply it

Larry is a three-month-old baby. His mother Lucy spends most time with him and is his main caregiver. Larry's father has often noticed how Larry and Lucy just seem to be 'in tune' with each other when they are playing together.

Using the concepts of reciprocity and interactional synchrony, explain what sort of behaviours you would expect to see from Larry and Lucy.

Reciprocity and interactional synchrony

Early interactions are meaningful.	From a very early age babies and caregivers have intense and meaningful interactions.
	The quality of these interactions is associated with the successful development of attachments.
	Two kinds of interaction: reciprocity (taking turns to respond) and interactional synchrony (simultaneous imitation).

Reciprocity

Interactions involve *reciprocity*.	Reciprocity is achieved when baby and caregiver respond to and elicit responses from each other.
	For example, a caregiver responds to a baby's smile by saying something, and then the baby responds by making some sounds of pleasure.
Alert phases are times for interaction.	Mothers successfully respond around two-thirds of the time (Feldman and Eidelman 2007).
	From around three months this interaction becomes more intense and reciprocal.
Babies have an active role.	Traditional views of childhood have seen the baby in a passive role, receiving care from an adult.
	However it seems that babies are active participants. Both caregiver and baby can initiate interactions and take turns to do so.

Interactional synchrony

Interactions involve *synchrony*.	People are said to be synchronised when they carry out the same actions simultaneously.
	A formal definition is 'the temporal co-ordination of micro-level social behaviour' (Feldman 2007), e.g. caregiver and baby mirror each others' behaviour.
The beginnings of interactional synchrony.	Meltzoff and Moore (1977) observed the beginnings of interactional synchrony in babies as young as two weeks old.
	Adult displayed one of three facial expressions or one of three gestures. Filmed the baby's response.
	Babies' expression and gestures were more likely to mirror those of the adults than chance would predict.
Importance for attachment.	Isabella *et al.* (1989) observed 30 mothers and babies together and assessed the degree of synchrony.
	The researchers also assessed the quality of mother–baby attachment.
	They found that high levels of synchrony were associated with better quality mother–baby attachment (e.g. the emotional intensity of the relationship).

One strength of the research on this topic is the use of filmed observations.

Mother–baby interactions are usually filmed, often from multiple angles. Very fine details of behaviour can be recorded and analysed later.

Also babies don't know they are being observed, so their behaviour does not change in response to observation (generally the main problem for observational research).

This means the studies have good **reliability** and **validity**.

Interactional synchrony has been described as being like a 'dance' between parent and child.

Revision BOOSTER

Every AO3 page of this book includes a summary sentence to round off each evaluation. They often begin with a phrase such as, 'This means that...' or 'Therefore we can see...' Try and get into the habit of doing likewise. You don't have to use this exact wording, but the benefits of this kind of language are that it's evaluative and it makes your critical points crystal clear.

One limitation for the research is the difficulty in observing babies.

It is hard to observe babies' behaviour because they are not very co-ordinated. We just observe small gestures and small changes in expression.

It is also hard to interpret the meaning of babies' movements, e.g. deciding if a hand movement is a response to the caregiver or a random twitch.

This means we cannot be certain that any particular interactions observed between baby and caregiver are meaningful.

Another limitation is difficulty inferring developmental importance.

Feldman (2012) points out that synchrony (and reciprocity) simply describe behaviours that occur at the same time.

These are robust phenomena in the sense that they can be reliably observed, but this may not be useful as it does not tell us their purpose.

This means that we cannot be certain from observations that reciprocity or synchrony are important in development.

Counterpoint

There is some evidence from other sources, e.g. Isabella *et al.* (1989), to suggest that good levels of reciprocity and synchrony are associated with good quality attachments.

This means that, on balance, these early interactions are likely to have importance for development.

Evaluation extra: Practical value versus ethics.

Research into early interactions has allowed psychologists to improve the quality of caregiver–infant attachment, for example by Parent Child Interaction Therapy.

However, this kind of research is socially sensitive because it can be used to argue that mothers should focus just on interacting with their baby and not return to work.

This means that the practical value may be outweighed by its negative social consequences.

Do you agree with this conclusion?

Knowledge Check

1. Explain what is meant by 'reciprocity' **and** 'interactional synchrony' in the context of caregiver–infant interactions.
   (2 marks + 2 marks)

2. Briefly evaluate research into caregiver–infant interaction.
   (4 marks)

3. Outline research into reciprocity in humans. *(4 marks)*

4. Describe **and** evaluate research into caregiver–infant interactions in humans.
   (12 marks AS, 16 marks AL)

Schaffer's stages of attachment

Spec spotlight

Stages of attachment as identified by Schaffer. Multiple attachments.

6-week-old Nathan still hadn't worked out who his mum was – the large thing talking softly in his ear or the little yellow thing floating in the water.

Apply it

A child psychologist observes Larry's behaviour at several points throughout his first year, and makes the following notes:

- *Larry becomes very upset when he sees a stranger and can only be comforted by his mum.*
- *Larry grasps every object presented to him, from mummy's finger to his teddy bear. He makes the same gurgling noises at everyone he sees.*
- *Larry seems to recognise other family members (such as his grandparents) and is happy to play with them all.*
- *When Larry cries, he is happy to be comforted by family friends and even babysitters as well as his mum and dad.*

1. Identify which stages of Larry's development are being described.
2. Explain your choices and give Larry's approximate age at each stage.

Stages of attachment

Stage 1: *Asocial stage* (first few weeks).	Baby's behaviour towards people and inanimate objects is quite similar. Some preference for familiar people (more easily calmed by them). Babies are also happier in the presence of other people.
Stage 2: *Indiscriminate attachment* (2–7 months).	Babies now display more observable social behaviour, with a preference for people rather than inanimate objects. They recognise and prefer familiar people. Babies do not show *stranger* or *separation anxiety*. Attachment is indiscriminate because it's the same towards all.
Stage 3: *Specific attachment* (from around 7 months).	Stranger anxiety and separation anxiety when separated from one particular person. Baby is said to have formed a specific attachment with the *primary attachment figure*. This is in most cases the person who offers the most interaction and responds to the baby's 'signals' with the most skill (the mother in 65% of cases).
Stage 4: *Multiple attachments* (by one year).	*Secondary attachments* with other adults form shortly after. In Schaffer and Emerson's study, 29% of babies had secondary (multiple) attachments within a month of forming a primary (specific) attachment. By the age of one year the majority of infants had multiple secondary attachments.

Schaffer and Emerson (1964) Stages of attachment

PROCEDURE	60 babies from Glasgow, most from working-class families. Researchers visited babies and mothers at home every month for a year and again at 18 months.
	Separation anxiety measured by asking mothers about their children's behaviour during everyday separations (e.g. adult leaving the room). *Stranger anxiety* was measured by asking mothers questions about their children's anxiety response to unfamiliar adults.
FINDINGS AND CONCLUSIONS	Babies developed attachments through a sequence of stages, from asocial through to a specific attachment to multiple attachments – as outlined above.
	The specific attachment tended to be to the person who was most interactive and sensitive to babies' signals and facial expressions (i.e. *reciprocity*). This was not necessarily the person the baby spent most time with.

One strength of Schaffer and Emerson's study is that it has external validity.

Most of the observations (not stranger anxiety) were made by parents during ordinary activities and reported to researchers.

The alternative would be to have observers present in the babies' homes. This may have distracted the babies or made them feel more anxious.

This means it is highly likely that the participants behaved naturally while being observed.

Counterpoint

Mothers may have been biased in what they reported, e.g. they might not have noticed when their baby was showing signs of anxiety or may have misremembered it.

This means that even if babies behaved naturally their behaviour may not have been accurately recorded.

One limitation is poor evidence for the asocial stage.

Because of their stage of physical development young babies have poor co-ordination and are fairly immobile.

This makes it difficult for mothers to accurately report signs of anxiety and attachment for this age group.

This means the babies might actually be quite social but, because of flawed methods, they appear to be asocial.

Another strength is real-world application to day care.

In the early stages (asocial and indiscriminate attachments) babies can be comforted by any skilled adult.

But if a child starts day care later, during the stage of specific attachments, care from an unfamiliar adult may cause distress and longer-term problems.

This means that Schaffer and Emerson's stages can help parents making day care decisions.

These ears demean us both.

Evaluation extra: Generalisability.

Schaffer and Emerson based their stages on a single but large-scale study of babies' development conducted in working-class Glasgow.

However, child-rearing practices vary considerably according to cultural and historical context e.g. multiple attachments the norm in **collectivist** cultures (van IJzendoorn 1993).

This means that some of the observations from this study may not **generalise** to other populations.

Revision BOOSTER

Remember mnemonics? (page 36) They can help you remember basic facts. Schaffer's stages of attachment is a perfect topic for this.

Take the first letter of each stage (A, I, S, M) and construct a sentence of four words, each beginning with one of these letters, in order.

Or, include each word in full (and in order) in a longer sentence (more of a challenge this one, but could be even more memorable).

Knowledge Check

1. Explain what is meant by 'multiple attachments'.
   (2 marks)
2. Outline Schaffer's stages of attachment. *(6 marks)*
3. Explain **one** strength **and one** limitation of Schaffer's stages of attachment.
   (3 marks + 3 marks)
4. Outline what research has shown about multiple attachments. *(4 marks)*
5. Discuss the stages of attachment identified by Schaffer.
   (12 marks AS, 16 marks AL)
6. Describe **and** evaluate research into multiple attachments.
   (12 marks AS, 16 marks AL)

The role of the father

Spec spotlight

The role of the father.

Research suggests that fathers can play an important role in their child's development. No excuse for the matching outfits though.

Caregiver versus attachment figure

There is a difference between a primary caregiver and a primary attachment figure. A primary caregiver is the person who spends most time with a baby, caring for its needs. A primary attachment figure is the person to whom the baby has the strongest attachment. Often the same person fulfils the two roles but not always.

Revision BOOSTER

You will notice that there are usually six key points for every approach. This would cover what you would need in any essay in terms of descriptive content (both for AS and A level essays because the description is always just 6 marks). Don't be tempted to overdescribe.

'Primary' attachments are more about emotional closeness and a basis for later emotional development.

Role of the father	
Primary attachment usually with mothers but sometimes both.	Schaffer and Emerson (1964) found that the majority of babies became attached to their mother first (this happens around 7 months).
	In only 3% of cases the father was the first sole object of attachment.
	In 27% of cases the father was the joint first object of attachment with the mother.
75% eventually form *secondary attachments* with father.	In 75% of babies studied an attachment was formed with the father by the age of 18 months.
	This was indicated by the fact the babies protested when their father walked away, a sign of attachment.
A distinctive role for the father.	Grossmann et al. (2002) carried out a **longitudinal** study looking at parents' behaviour and its relationship to the quality of children's attachments into their teens.
	This research found that quality of attachment with the father was less important for adolescent attachment than the quality of attachment with the mother.
	Therefore fathers may be less important in long-term emotional development.
	However, Grossmann et al. also found that the quality of fathers' play with babies was related to quality of adolescent attachments.
	This suggests that fathers have a different role in attachment, one that is more to do with play and stimulation and less to do with emotional care.
Fathers can be primary attachment figures.	Some evidence suggests that when fathers do take on the role of being the main caregiver they adopt behaviours more typical of mothers.
	Field (1978) filmed 4-month-old babies and found that primary caregiver fathers, like mothers, spent more time smiling, imitating and holding babies than secondary caregiver fathers.
	These behaviours are related to interactional synchrony and the formation of an emotional attachment (Isabella et al. 1989).
Level of response is most important.	Smiling, imitating and holding babies (interactional synchrony) are behaviours that are important in building a primary (emotional) attachment with a baby.
	So it seems the father can be the more 'emotional' attachment figure.
	The key to the attachment relationship is the level of responsiveness not the gender of the parent.

One limitation is confusion over research questions.

Some psychologists want to understand the role of fathers as secondary attachment figures. But others are more concerned with fathers as a primary attachment figure.

The former have tended to see fathers as behaving differently from mothers and having a distinct role. The latter have found that fathers can take on a 'maternal' role.

This means psychologists cannot easily answer the simple question: what is the role of the father?

One limitation is conflicting evidence from different methodologies.

Grossmann *et al.* (2002) suggest fathers have a distinct role in children's development, involving play and stimulation.

However, McCallum and Golombok (2004) found that children without a father do not develop differently.

This means the question of whether fathers have a distinctive role remains unanswered.

Counterpoint

Findings may not be in conflict. Fathers may typically take on particular roles in two-parent heterosexual families. Other family structures adapt to not having fathers.

This means that findings may be clear after all – there may be a distinctive role for fathers when present, but families adapt to not having one.

One strength is using findings in parenting advice.

Mothers may feel pressured to stay at home and fathers to focus on work. This may not be the best solution for all families.

Research on the flexibility of the role of the father can be used to offer reassuring advice to parents.

This means that parental anxiety about the role of fathers can be reduced and parenting decisions made easier.

Evaluation extra: Bias in this research.

Preconceptions about how fathers behave are created by discussions about mothers' and fathers' parenting behaviour.

Stereotypes (e.g. fathers are more playful) may cause observer bias and lead to inaccurate observations.

This means that observational studies of fathers may lack **validity** and conclusions cannot be trusted.

Apply it

Larry is now eight months old. His dad is much more involved with his son, playing with him regularly every day. But recently he's noticed that Larry tends to go to his mother for comfort when he is distressed, so Larry's father sometimes feels a bit left out and worries that he's not being a 'proper' dad.

Using psychological research, explain why Larry's dad has no need to worry.

Revision BOOSTER

On the left we have identified FOUR evaluation points and for each we have provided THREE levels of elaboration (plus ONE counterpoint).

On page 6 we suggested there are two routes for doing evaluation in an AS essay (6 marks AO3) – either do two or three points that are WELL-ELABORATED or more points with less elaboration.

Attachment research within this area may be affected by stereotyped assumptions about the roles of mothers and fathers.

Knowledge Check

1. Briefly explain the role of the father in attachment. *(3 marks)*
2. Explain what research has shown about the role of the father in attachment. *(6 marks)*
3. Discuss the role of the father in attachment.
   (12 marks AS, 16 marks AL)

Animal studies of attachment

Spec spotlight

Animal studies of attachment: Lorenz and Harlow.

For fans of goslings everywhere.

Revision BOOSTER

This topic illustrates the importance of thorough revision. That's because you may have to write about any of these: Harlow's animal research only, Lorenz's animal research only, both Harlow's and Lorenz's research, animal research into attachment in general. Don't be tempted to gamble with your revision and leave gaps. Be clear in your own mind about what you will include for each possibility.

Lorenz (1952) Imprinting

PROCEDURE

Konrad Lorenz randomly divided a large clutch of goose eggs:
- One half were hatched with the mother goose in their natural environment.
- The other half hatched in an incubator where the first moving object they saw was Lorenz.

Mixed all goslings together to see whom they would follow.

Lorenz also observed birds and their later courtship behaviour.

FINDINGS AND CONCLUSIONS

Incubator group followed Lorenz, **control group** followed the mother.

Lorenz identified a *critical period* in which *imprinting* needs to take place, e.g. few hours after hatching.
If imprinting did not occur within that time, chicks did not attach themselves to the mother figure.

Sexual imprinting also occurs whereby the birds acquire a template of the desirable characteristics required in a mate.

Harlow (1958) Importance of contact comfort

PROCEDURE

Harry Harlow reared 16 rhesus monkeys with two wire model 'mothers' (see picture below left):
- Condition 1 – milk was dispensed by the plain-wire 'mother'.
- Condition 2 – milk was dispensed by the cloth-covered 'mother'.

The monkeys' preferences were measured.

To measure attachment-like behaviour, Harlow observed how the monkeys reacted when placed in frightening situations. For example, Harlow added a noisy mechanical teddy bear to the environment.

Harlow and his colleagues also continued to study the monkeys who had been deprived of their 'real' mother into adulthood.

FINDINGS AND CONCLUSIONS

Baby monkeys cuddled the cloth-covered mother in preference to the plain-wire mother regardless of which dispensed milk. This suggests that contact comfort was of more importance than food when it came to attachment behaviour.

The monkeys sought comfort from the cloth-covered mother when frightened.

As adults, the monkeys who had been deprived of their real mothers suffered severe consequences – they were more aggressive, less sociable and less skilled in mating than other monkeys.

One strength is support for the concept of imprinting.

Regolin and Vallortigara (1995) exposed chicks to simple shape-combinations that moved.	When shown a range of moving shapes the chicks followed these in preference to other shapes.	This suggests that young animals are born with an innate mechanism to imprint on a moving object.

One limitation is generalising from birds to humans.

The mammalian attachment system is quite different from imprinting in birds.	For example, mammalian mothers show more emotional attachment to their young.	This means that it may not be appropriate to **generalise** Lorenz's ideas about imprinting to humans.

Evaluation extra: Applications to human behaviour.

The concept of imprinting can explain some human behaviour.	For example 'baby duck syndrome', in which computer users become attached to their first operating system.	This means that imprinting is a meaningful process in humans as well as birds.

Well hello, lover...

Apply it

A film called Winged Migration *was made using Canada geese (and other bird species). Human handlers wore high-visibility jackets and made goose-like honking noises. The goslings followed them around almost immediately after they hatched.*

Use Lorenz's research to explain why the goslings behaved in this way.

One strength is that Harlow's research has real-world value.

It has helped social workers understand risk factors in child abuse and thus intervene to prevent it (Howe 1998).	We also now understand the importance of attachment figures for baby monkeys in zoos and breeding programmes.	This means that Harlow's research has benefitted both animals and humans.

One limitation is generalising from monkeys to humans.

Monkeys are clearly more similar to humans than Lorenz's geese, and all mammals share some similarities in their attachment systems.	However they are not human and in some ways the human mind and behaviour are much more complex.	This means that it may not be appropriate to generalise Harlow's findings to humans.

Rhesus monkeys.

Knowledge Check

1. Describe the findings **and** procedures of **one** animal study of attachment. *(6 marks)*
2. Outline how Lorenz **and** Harlow studied attachment using animals. *(6 marks)*
3. Briefly evaluate **either** Lorenz's **or** Harlow's animal studies of attachment. *(6 marks)*
4. Outline **and** evaluate **two** animal studies of attachment. *(12 marks AS, 16 marks AL)*

Evaluation extra: Ethical issues.

Harlow's procedures caused severe long-term distress to his monkey participants, though the research led to useful applications.	However, his findings and conclusions have important theoretical and practical applications.	This suggests that, in spite of its benefits, Harlow's research perhaps should not have been carried out.

Explanations of attachment: Learning theory

Spec spotlight

Explanations of attachment: learning theory.

'Learning theory' is explained on page 72. It is the theory proposed by behaviourists (the behaviourist approach).

Classical conditioning of attachment

Unconditioned stimulus (UCS) →	Unconditioned response (UCR)
Food	Pleasure
Neutral stimulus (NS) →	No response
Caregiver	
UCS + NS →	UCR
Food + Caregiver	Pleasure
Conditioned stimulus (CS) →	Conditioned response (CR)
Caregiver	Pleasure

Despite appearances, Frank loved playing the spoons.

Revision BOOSTER

Never fall into the trap of writing in general terms about learning theory (e.g. a non-specific description of classical conditioning). In the case of attachment, you have to apply learning theory to explain the development of caregiver–infant attachment.

The general rule is this – if you don't mention attachment throughout your answer then your answer is likely to gain very little credit.

Dollard and Miller (1950) Learning theory of attachment

Importance of food.	This is sometimes called the 'cupboard love' explanation because it emphasises the importance of food in attachment formation. Children learn to love whoever feeds them.
Role of classical conditioning.	**Classical conditioning** involves learning to associate two stimuli. In attachment: **UCS** (food) leads to **UCR** (a feeling of pleasure). This response is not learned so it is an **unconditioned response** (unlearned).
Baby learns that mother produces a sense of pleasure.	A caregiver (e.g. mother) starts as a **NS**, i.e. something that produces no response. However, when the caregiver provides food over time, he/she becomes associated with 'food'. So the neutral stimulus becomes a **CS**. Once conditioning has taken place the sight of the caregiver produces a **CR** of pleasure. According to a learning theorist, the conditioned pleasure response is the basis of love. Now an attachment has formed and the caregiver becomes an *attachment figure*.
Role of operant conditioning.	**Operant conditioning** explains why babies cry for comfort (an important building block for attachment). Crying leads to a response from the caregiver (e.g. feeding). As long as the caregiver provides the correct response, crying is reinforced because it produces a pleasurable consequence.
Negative reinforcement.	At the same time as the baby is reinforced for crying, the caregiver receives *negative reinforcement* because the crying stops (negative reinforcement is escaping from something unpleasant, which is reinforcing). This interplay of positive/negative reinforcement strengthens an attachment.
Drive reduction.	Hunger is a *primary drive*, an innate biological motivator. We are motivated to eat to reduce the hunger drive. Attachment is a *secondary drive* learned by an association between the caregiver and the satisfaction of a primary drive. Sears *et al.* (1957) suggested that, as caregivers provide food, the primary drive of hunger becomes **generalised** to them.

One limitation of learning theory is counter-evidence from animal studies.

Lorenz's geese imprinted on the first moving object they saw. Harlow's monkeys attached to a soft surrogate in preference to a wire one with milk.

In both these animal studies, imprinting/attachment did not develop as a result of feeding.

This shows that factors other than feeding are important in attachment formation.

Another limitation is counter-evidence from human studies.

Schaffer and Emerson (1964) showed that for many babies their main attachment was not to the person who fed them.

Also, Isabella et al. (1989) found that interactional synchrony (unrelated to feeding) predicted attachment quality.

This again suggests that other factors are more important in attachment formation than feeding.

Cupboard love. Actually that looks more like a wardrobe.

One strength is that some elements of conditioning could still be involved.

It seems unlikely that association with food is central to attachment. However, conditioning may still play some role in attachment.

For example a baby's choice of primary attachment figure may be determined by the fact that a caregiver becomes associated with warmth and comfort.

This means that conditioning could still be important in choice of attachment figures, though not the process of attachment formation.

Counterpoint

However, this point of view ignores the fact that babies take a very active role in the interactions that produce attachment. For example they initiate interactions (Feldman and Eidelman 2007).

This suggests that learning theory may be inappropriate in explaining *any* aspect of attachment.

Apply it

Margarita is four weeks old and her mum Yvette is her primary caregiver. Yvette prefers to be the one to wake up in the night and feed Margarita, as well as at all other times of the day because she's on maternity leave from work. Margarita's dad Aaron spends just as much time with her, doing the fun stuff like playing. But he's worried that his attachment bond with Margarita won't be as secure as Yvette's.

1. Look at all of the evidence on this spread. Explain in terms of learning theory why Aaron is concerned.

2. What would you say to him to address his concerns?

Evaluation extra: Social learning theory.

Hay and Vespo (1988) suggest that parents teach children to love them by **modelling** attachment behaviour e.g. hugging and kissing.

Parents also reward babies with approval when they display their own attachment behaviour ('that's a lovely smile', etc).

This means that social learning theory can provide better explanations, including explaining the active role taken by babies in attachment development.

Knowledge Check

1. Describe the learning theory of attachment. *(4 marks)*

2. Outline **two** limitations of the learning theory of attachment. *(3 marks + 3 marks)*

3. Discuss the learning theory of attachment. *(12 marks AS, 16 marks AL)*

Explanations of attachment: Bowlby's theory

Spec spotlight

Explanations of attachment: Bowlby's monotropic theory. The concepts of a critical period and an internal working model.

Most babies form attachments with several caregivers – although they don't usually have a shared dress code.

Revision BOOSTER

Bowlby's theory often provokes strong feelings because it touches on the issue of who is best equipped to look after babies (i.e. is it always the mother?).

It's perfectly OK for you to have strong opinions on this (and any) issue. But don't allow your personal beliefs to colour your judgement when writing about Bowlby's theory. It's not acceptable to say, 'Bowlby was a sexist pig because he believed that a woman's place is in the home'. But it is acceptable (highly desirable in fact) to evaluate his theory rationally in terms of the evidence.

Bowlby (1958, 1969) Monotropic theory

Attachment is innate, like imprinting.	Bowlby gave an evolutionary explanation – that attachment is an innate system that gives a survival advantage.
	Imprinting and attachment evolved because they ensure young animals stay close to their caregivers and this protects them from hazards.
Monotropic = having a *primary attachment figure*.	Bowlby's theory is described as monotropic because of the emphasis on the child's attachment to one caregiver (mono = 'one' and tropic = 'leaning towards'). This attachment is different from others and more important.
	Bowlby believed that the more time a baby spent with this primary attachment figure / mother-figure (not necessarily the biological mother, or indeed a female) the better. There are two main reasons:
	(1) *Law of continuity* – the more constant a child's care, the better the quality of attachment.
	(2) *Law of accumulated separation* – the effects of every separation add up. So, 'the safest dose is therefore a zero dose'.
Babies are born with *social releasers*.	Bowlby suggested that babies are born with a set of innate 'cute' behaviours (e.g. smiling, cooing, gripping) that encourage attention from adults.
	The purpose of these social releasers is to activate adult social interaction (i.e. make an adult attach to the baby); Bowlby recognised that attachment is a reciprocal system.
There is a *critical period*.	Bowlby proposed that there is a critical period of about two years when the infant attachment system is active. In fact, he viewed this as more of a *sensitive period*.
	A child is maximally sensitive at 6 months and this may extend up to the age of 2 years. If an attachment has not formed in this time, a child will find it much harder to form one later.
The first attachment forms an *internal working model* of relationships.	Bowlby argued that the child forms a mental representation (internal working model) of the relationship with their primary attachment figure. This internal working model serves as a 'template' for what relationships are like.
	A child whose first experience is a loving relationship with a reliable caregiver will tend to form an expectation that all relationships are loving and reliable. However, a child whose first relationship involves poor treatment may expect such treatment from others.
	The internal working model may also affect the child's later ability to be a parent themselves.

One limitation is that the concept of monotropy lacks validity.

The relationship with the primary attachment figure may simply be *stronger* than other attachments, rather than *different* in quality, as Bowlby believed.

Other family members may well develop attachments with the baby that have the same qualities, such as comfort and a secure base from which to explore.

This means that Bowlby may have been wrong to suggest that there is a unique quality to a child's primary attachment.

One strength is evidence supporting the role of social releasers.

Brazelton *et al.* (1975) instructed primary attachment figures to ignore their babies' social releasers.

Babies (who were previously shown to be normally responsive) initially showed some distress, but eventually some curled up and lay motionless.

This supports the idea that social releasers play an important role in attachment development.

Another strength is support for the idea of the internal working model.

The idea of the internal working model predicts that patterns of attachment will be passed from one generation to the next.

Bailey *et al.* (2007) studied 99 mothers. Those with poor attachment to their own parents were more likely to have one-year-olds who were poorly attached.

This supports Bowlby's idea of an internal working model of attachment as it is being passed through families.

Counterpoint

There are other influences on social development. For example a baby's genetically-influenced personality is important in the development of social behaviour, including their later parenting style.

This suggests that Bowlby overemphasised the importance of the internal working model in development.

Evaluation extra: Feminist concerns.

The laws of continuity and accumulated separation imply that working mothers may damage their baby's development (Burman 1994).

However Bowlby's theory did draw attention to a mother's importance and also had real-world applications (e.g. day care).

This means that, although Bowlby's theory has had important applications, it may also have contributed to the oppression of women, particularly working mothers.

Apply it

Eddie is six months old. His mum died not long after he was born and his dad is his primary caregiver who takes good care of all his needs.

Camelia is 18 months old. She has always lived in an orphanage where 'care' is provided by several different staff members. New staff come and go on a regular basis.

Leah is four years old. She was physically abused by her biological parents for the first two years of her life, but is now being adopted into a very caring and loving home.

1. Use Bowlby's theory and the concepts described on this spread to explain the quality of attachments you would expect to find in these three cases.

2. Do you predict Eddie, Camelia or Leah will be most likely to go on to be a successful parent themselves? Explain your choice.

Knowledge Check

1. Explain what is meant by 'critical period' **and** 'internal working model'.
(*2 marks + 2 marks*)

2. Outline Bowlby's monotropic theory of attachment. (*6 marks*)

3. Briefly evaluate Bowlby's monotropic theory of attachment. (*4 marks*)

4. Discuss Bowlby's monotropic theory of attachment.
(*12 marks AS, 16 marks AL*)

Chapter 3: Attachment

Spec spotlight

Ainsworth's 'Strange Situation'.
Types of attachment: secure,
insecure–avoidant and
insecure–resistant.

A dog playing a violin – now that's what I call a strange situation.

Apply it

Three babies

Nell likes to be with her mum but is happy to play elsewhere in the room. However, she does keep one eye on where her mum is, and gets a bit upset if her mum is out of the room for a long time.

Sunny clings to his mum a lot and likes to be carried around. His mum finds it difficult to put Sunny down for any length of time without him becoming distressed.

Gennady doesn't seem to mind whether his mum is there or not. He hardly notices if she leaves the room, and he doesn't show any inclination to be with her when she returns.

1. Identify each baby's attachment type **and** explain your decisions.

2. What other behaviours would you expect to observe in each baby?

Ainsworth and Bell (1970) The 'Strange Situation'

PROCEDURE

Ainsworth and Bell (1970) developed the Strange Situation as a method to assess the quality of a baby's attachment to a caregiver.

It is a *controlled observation* procedure in a lab (a controlled environment) with a two-way mirror through which psychologists can observe a baby's behaviour.

Five categories are used to judge attachment quality:

1. Proximity-seeking – well-attached babies stay close to caregiver.
2. Exploration and secure-base behaviour – good attachment makes a baby confident to explore, using the caregiver as point of safety.
3. Stranger anxiety – displayed by well-attached babies.
4. Separation anxiety – displayed by well-attached babies.
5. Response to reunion with the caregiver after separation for a short period of time – well-attached babies are enthusiastic.

The procedure has seven 'episodes', each lasting three minutes.

1. Baby is encouraged to explore by caregiver.
2. Stranger enters and talks to caregiver, approaches baby.
3. Caregiver leaves.
4. Caregiver returns, stranger leaves.
5. Caregiver leaves baby alone.
6. Stranger returns.
7. Caregiver returns.

FINDINGS AND CONCLUSIONS

Ainsworth and Bell found distinct patterns in the way babies behaved. They identified three main types of attachment.

Secure attachment (Type B: 60–75% of British toddlers):

- Baby happy to explore but seeks proximity to caregiver (secure base).
- Shows moderate separation anxiety and stranger anxiety.
- Requires and accepts comfort from caregiver on reunion.

Insecure–avoidant attachment (Type A: 20–25% of British toddlers):

- Baby explores freely but does not seek proximity (no secure base).
- Shows little/no separation and stranger anxiety.
- Avoids contact at the reunion stage.

Insecure–resistant attachment (Type C: 3% of British toddlers):

- Baby explores less and seeks greater proximity.
- Shows considerable stranger and separation anxiety.
- Resists comfort when reunited with caregiver.

One strength is the Strange Situation has good predictive validity.

Attachment type predicts later development. For example, secure babies typically have greater success at school (McCormick *et al.* 2016).

In contrast, insecure–resistant attachment is associated with the worst outcomes, e.g. bullying (Kokkinos 2007) and adult mental health problems (Ward *et al.* 2006).

This is evidence for the validity of the concept because it can explain (predict) future outcomes.

Counterpoint

Although the Strange Situation measures something that predicts later development, it may be measuring genetic differences in anxiety (Kagan 1982).

This means the Strange Situation may not actually measure attachment.

Another strength is the Strange Situation has good inter-rater reliability.

Different observers watching the same babies generally agree on attachment type. Bick *et al.* (2012) found 94% agreement in one team.

This may be because the Strange Situation takes place under controlled conditions and because the behavioural categories are easy to observe.

This means that we can be confident that the attachment type of a baby identified in the Strange Situation does not just depend on who is observing them.

One limitation is that the Strange Situation may be a culture-bound test.

The Strange Situation test might not have the same meaning in countries outside Europe and the US where it was created.

Cultural differences in children's experiences mean they respond differently, e.g. Japanese babies show anxiety because they are not used to being left by caregiver (Takahashi 1986).

This means it is difficult to know what the Strange Situation is measuring in some countries/cultures.

Evaluation extra: Other attachment types.

Main and Solomon (1986) identified a fourth category of attachment – disorganised (Type D), a mix of resistant and avoidant behaviours.

However, Type D babies are unusual and have generally experienced some form of severe neglect or abuse, associated with later psychological disorders.

This means that Ainsworth's classification is adequate as a description of *normal* variations in attachment.

Revision BOOSTER

Here's one way to help you remember the behaviours associated with different attachment types. Draw up a table with columns for 'Secure', 'Insecure–avoidant' and 'Insecure–resistant', and rows for 'Proximity-seeking', 'Exploration/secure base', 'Stranger anxiety', 'Separation anxiety' and 'Response on reunion'.

Complete the table using words such as 'strong', 'high' and so on.

'Are you not getting this, mum and dad?! I am insecure–resistant!!'

Knowledge Check

1. Explain what is meant by 'secure', 'insecure–avoidant' **and** 'insecure–resistant'.
   (2 marks + 2 marks + 2 marks)

2. Ainsworth identified three types of attachment. Choose any **two** types and explain **one** difference between them. *(3 marks)*

3. Outline how Ainsworth studied types of attachment. *(6 marks)*

4. Explain **one or more** strengths of Ainsworth's Strange Situation. *(4 marks)*

5. Describe **and** evaluate research into types of attachment. *(12 marks AS, 16 marks AL)*

Cultural variations in attachment

Spec spotlight

Cultural variations in attachment, including van IJzendoorn.

One of the key influences on behaviour is culture. Psychologists often make a broad distinction between individualist and collectivist cultures, or Western/ non-Western and industrialised/ non-industrialised countries/ cultures. However any attempt to divide the world into polar opposites cannot truly reflect the differences that exist between cultures.

'I just need to learn the study by van Iz ... van Izen ... van Oozen ... van Izling ...aw – I give up.'

Psychology student Neville wasn't renowned for his cultural sensitivity.

Revision BOOSTER

In an exam question you may have to describe the procedures and findings of studies, or just one of them. For example, van IJzendoorn is specifically mentioned in the specification, so you need to be thoroughly familiar with all aspects of what he did and what he found in his research.

Alternatively, you might have to write about 'research', a term which gives you more flexibility because it doesn't tie you to one specific study or aspect of a study (and can even include theories, if there are any relevant to the topic).

van IJzendoorn and Kroonenberg (1988) Meta-analysis

PROCEDURE

The researchers looked at the proportions of *secure, insecure–avoidant* and *insecure–resistant attachments* across a range of countries.

They also looked at the differences within the same countries to get an idea of variations within a culture.

They found 32 studies of attachment where the Strange Situation had been used. These were conducted in eight countries, 15 in the US. Overall the studies yielded results for 1,990 children.

The data was **meta-analysed**, results being combined and weighted for sample size.

FINDINGS AND CONCLUSIONS

Secure attachment was the most common classification in all countries, but ranged from 50% in China to 75% in Britain.

In **individualist** cultures rates of insecure–resistant attachment were similar to Ainsworth's original sample (all under 14%) but this was not true for the **collectivist** samples from China, Japan and Israel where rates were above 25% (and where rates of *insecure–avoidant attachment* were reduced).

This suggests that there were cultural differences in the distribution of insecure attachment.

Variations between results of studies *within* the same country were actually 150% greater than those *between* countries.

In the US, one study found 46% securely attached compared to one sample as high as 90%.

Other studies

PROCEDURE

Simonelli *et al.* (2014) assessed 76 babies aged 12 months in Italy using the Strange Situation to see whether the proportion of attachment types still matched previous studies in Italy.

Jin *et al.* (2012) compared the attachment types of 87 Korean babies to proportions in other studies.

FINDINGS AND CONCLUSIONS

Simonelli *et al.* found that 50% were secure, with 36% insecure– avoidant. This lower rate of secure attachment may be because increasingly mothers work long hours and use more childcare. This shows that cultural changes can affect patterns of attachment.

Jin *et al.* found similar patterns of secure and insecure attachment to other studies. However within insecure categories there were differences – only one baby was avoidant. This pattern is similar to Japan and may be because both countries have similar child-rearing practices.

One strength of the studies is the use of indigenous researchers.

Indigenous researchers are those from the same cultural background as the participants, e.g. Grossmann et al. (1981) – Germans working with German participants.

Using indigenous researchers aids communication between researchers and participants and helps prevent misunderstandings e.g. of instructions.

This means that there is an excellent chance that researchers and participants communicated successfully, increasing the **validity** of the study.

Counterpoint

This has not been true of all cross-cultural attachment research, e.g. Americans Morelli and Tronick (1991) investigated the Efé in Zaire.

This means that some cross-cultural attachment research may have communication errors and hence lacks validity.

One limitation is the impact of confounding variables.

Studies conducted in different countries may not be matched for sample characteristics, e.g. studies in different countries may use children of different ages and social classes.

Environmental variables may also differ, e.g. using smaller rooms which might encourage babies to explore more.

This means that studies assessing attachment types carried out in different countries may tell us little about cultural differences in attachment.

Another limitation is imposing a test designed in one culture (an imposed etic).

Using a test (the Strange Situation) in a different cultural context from the one for which is was designed may be meaningless.

The Strange Situation was designed in the US where lack of affection at reunion represents insecure attachment. However in Germany it would be seen as a sign of independence.

This means that it may be meaningless to compare attachment behaviours across countries.

Do you agree with this conclusion?

Evaluation extra: Competing explanations.

The reasons for similar patterns of attachment across cultures is explained by Bowlby's theory that attachment is innate, so secure attachment is the universal norm.

However van IJzendoorn and Kroonenberg suggest this similarity may be more a product of media representations of correct parenting.

This means that it is hard to know whether Bowlby's theory is true as there is a credible alternative explanation.

Oh dear, someone's not happy... The Strange Situation is not measuring what it claims to measure.

Knowledge Check

1. Explain what is meant by 'cultural variations' in attachment. *(2 marks)*
2. Outline van IJzendoorn's research into cultural variations in attachment. *(4 marks)*
3. Outline what research has found out about cultural variations in attachment. *(4 marks)*
4. Discuss what research has shown about cultural variations in attachment. *(12 marks AS, 16 marks AL)*

Bowlby's theory of maternal deprivation

Spec spotlight

Bowlby's theory of maternal deprivation.

Bowlby's mother-love pills – take several times a day for healthy development.

Revision BOOSTER

There is some overlap between topics within this chapter. First of all the overlap between this theory and Bowlby's monotropic theory of attachment (see page 58). It is important to make sure that you do not muddle the two – one is about the positive effects of attachment, the other is about the negative effects of emotional deprivation.

Another topic that overlaps with maternal deprivation is the research into the effects of institutionalisation on Romanian orphans (next spread). You can use this as an AO3 point. The key is to make your evaluation effective by explaining what the research tells us about Bowlby's theory, not by describing the research itself (that wouldn't be relevant).

Bowlby (1951) Theory of maternal deprivation

Continued emotional care is essential.	Continuous emotional (maternal) care from a mother or mother-substitute is necessary for normal emotional and intellectual development.
Separation may lead to *maternal deprivation*.	Bowlby believed that mother-love in infancy is 'as important for mental health as are vitamins and proteins for physical health'.
Separation is different from deprivation.	• Separation means the child not being physically in the presence of the primary attachment figure. • Deprivation means losing emotional care as a result of the separation. Deprivation can be avoided if alternative emotional care is offered, thus separation doesn't always cause deprivation.
Critical period of 2½ years.	If a child is separated from their mother (without substitute emotional care) for an extended time during the first 2½ years, then psychological damage is inevitable. There is a continuing risk up to the age of 5.
Intellectual development: lower IQ.	If a child is deprived of maternal care for too long during the critical period this may lead to mental retardation. Goldfarb (1947) found lower IQs in children from institutions compared to fostered children.
Emotional development: *affectionless psychopathy*.	Lack of emotional care may also lead to affectionless psychopathy – the inability to experience guilt or strong emotion towards others. This prevents the person developing normal relationships and is associated with criminality.

Bowlby (1944) 44 thieves study

PROCEDURE	The sample in this study was 44 delinquent teenagers accused of stealing.
	All 'thieves' were interviewed for signs of affectionless psychopathy: characterised by a lack of affection, guilt and empathy.
	Families were also interviewed to establish any prolonged separations from mothers.
FINDINGS AND CONCLUSIONS	14 of the 44 thieves could be described as affectionless psychopaths. 12 of these had experienced prolonged separation from their mothers in the first two years of their lives.
	In contrast only five of the remaining 30 'thieves' had experienced separations. This suggests prolonged early separation/deprivation caused affectionless psychopathy.

One limitation is that sources of evidence for maternal deprivation are flawed.

The 44 thieves study is flawed because it was open to bias – Bowlby himself assessed both deprivation and psychopathy, knowing what he hoped to find.

Also, Goldfarb's (1943) study of wartime orphans is flawed because he used traumatised participants who lacked good aftercare. This introduced **confounding variables**.

This means that Bowlby originally had no solid evidence on which to base his theory of maternal deprivation.

Counterpoint

There is some evidence from newer studies to support the theory of maternal deprivation. For example, Lévy et al. (2003) found that separating baby rats for one day had a permanent effect on their social development.

This means that there is now some evidence for the theory of maternal deprivation after all.

Another limitation is Bowlby confused deprivation and privation.

Rutter (1981) made the distinction between deprivation (separation from an attachment figure) and privation (failure to form an attachment) – privation has more serious effects.

The children Bowlby studied (e.g. the 44 thieves), and others he based his ideas on (e.g. Goldfarb's wartime orphans) may have been prived rather than deprived.

This means that Bowlby probably exaggerated the effects of deprivation on development.

A further limitation is the critical period is more of a sensitive period.

Koluchová (1976) conducted a **case study** of Czech twin boys isolated from age 18 months (locked in a cupboard). Later they were looked after by two loving adults and appeared to recover fully.

Shows that severe deprivation can have positive outcomes provided the child has some social interaction and good aftercare.

This means that the period identified by Bowlby may be a 'sensitive' one but it cannot be critical.

Evaluation extra: Conflicting evidence.

Replications of Bowlby's 44 thieves study (e.g. Lewis 1954) have generally failed to reproduce his findings on psychopathy.

However, some more recent research (e.g. Gao et al. 2010) has found links between poor maternal care and adult psychopathy.

This means the link between maternal deprivation and psychopathy are unclear.

Apply it

Skeels and Dye (1939) studied two groups of orphaned children aged 1–2. One group was raised in a home for 'mentally retarded' teenage girls and given one-to-one care (by the girls). The other group remained in an unstimulating orphanage without individual care. The children's intelligence (IQ) was tested at the start and the end of an 18-month period. The mean IQ of the one-to-one children had increased from 64.3 to 91.8 points. But in the orphanage children, the mean IQ decreased from 86.7 to 60.5 points.

Use Bowlby's theory of maternal deprivation to explain Skeels and Dye's results.

Bowlby thought that mother and baby should not be separated – even during business hours.

Knowledge Check

1. Explain what is meant by 'maternal deprivation'.
   (2 marks)

2. Outline Bowlby's theory of maternal deprivation. *(4 marks)*

3. Explain **one** strength **and one** limitation of Bowlby's theory of maternal deprivation.
   (3 marks + 3 marks)

4. Describe **and** evaluate Bowlby's theory of maternal deprivation.
   (12 marks AS, 16 marks AL)

Romanian orphan studies: Institutionalisation

Spec spotlight

Romanian orphan studies: effects of institutionalisation.

Institutionalised Romanian orphans. No joke.

Apply it

Tatiana began life in a Romanian orphanage but was adopted into a British family when she was just one year old. Now aged six years, she is being referred to an educational psychologist for two main reasons. Her performance at school is very poor, her reading and writing in particular – she finds even the basics difficult.

She also has serious behavioural problems, especially extreme attention-seeking – she is 'clingy' with everyone, even complete strangers.

Explain why Tatiana might be behaving in these ways. Refer to psychological research in your explanation.

Rutter *et al.* (2011) English and Romanian adoptee study (ERA)

PROCEDURE	The researchers have followed a group of 165 Romanian orphans who experienced very poor conditions before being adopted in the UK.
	This **longitudinal** study has tested the extent to which good care can make up for poor early experiences in institutions. Physical, **cognitive** and emotional development has been assessed at 4, 6, 11, 15 and 22–25 years.
	The study also followed a **control group** of 52 adopted children from the UK.
FINDINGS AND CONCLUSIONS	Half of the orphans showed delayed intellectual development when they came to the UK. At age 11 recovery rates were related to their age at adoption: • Those adopted before six months had a mean IQ of 102. • Those adopted after two years had a mean IQ of 77. These differences continued to be apparent at age 16 (Beckett *et al.* 2010).
	Frequency of *disinhibited attachment* related to the age at adoption. • Apparent in children adopted after they were six months old: clinginess, attention-seeking and indiscriminate affection to strangers. • Rare in children adopted before the age of six months.
	These findings support Bowlby's view that there is a *sensitive period* in the development of attachments – a failure to form an attachment before the age of six months (and after the age of 2 years) appears to have long-lasting effects.

Zeanah *et al.* (2005) Bucharest early intervention project (BEI)

PROCEDURE	The researchers used the Strange Situation to assess attachment in 95 Romanian children aged 12–31 months who had spent most of their lives in institutional care.
	They were compared to a control group of 50 children who had never experienced institutional care.
FINDINGS AND CONCLUSIONS	Only 19% of the institutionalised group were securely attached (74% of controls).
	44% of the institutionalised group had characteristics of disinhibited attachment (20% of the controls).

Effects of institutionalisation

Disinhibited attachment.	Such children tend to be equally friendly and affectionate towards people they know well or total strangers. This may be an adaptation to multiple caregivers.
Damage to intellectual development.	Institutionalised children often show signs of intellectual disability. This effect is not as pronounced if the children are adopted before 6 months of age.

One strength of the Romanian orphans study is real-world application.

Results from this research have led to improvements in the way children are cared for in institutions (Langton 2006).

Children's homes now avoid having large numbers of caregivers for each child. They have one or two 'key workers' who play a central role.

This means children in institutional care have a chance to develop normal attachments and disinhibited attachment is avoided.

Another strength is fewer confounding variables than other research.

There were many orphan studies before the Romanian orphans became available to study. These often involved children who experienced loss or trauma before they were institutionalised.

Neglect, abuse and bereavement meant it was hard to observe the effects of institutionalisation in isolation. The children were affected by multiple factors functioning as confounding variables.

This means we can be fairly sure that differences in institutionally-cared-for children are the result of this type of care (high internal validity).

Counterpoint

Romanian orphan studies may have new confounding variables because quality of care was so poor, making it hard to separate effects of institutional care from those of *poor* institutional care.

This means that internal validity might not be better than in previous studies after all.

One limitation is the lack of data on adult development.

It is too soon to say for certain whether children suffered permanent effects because we only have data on their development as far as their early twenties.

It will be some time before we have information about some key research questions (e.g. orphans' ability to form and maintain romantic and parenting relationships).

This means the Romanian orphan studies have not yet yielded their most important findings, some children may 'catch up'.

Evaluation extra: Social sensitivity.

Late-adopted children were shown to have low IQ. This might subsequently affect how they are treated by parents, teachers etc. and might create a self-fulfilling prophecy.

On the other hand, much has been learned from the Romanian orphan studies that might benefit future institutionalised or potentially institutionalised children.

So the potential benefits of the studies probably outweigh their social sensitivity.

Not everyone agrees with this conclusion. What do you think?

Research on institutionalisation led to key workers being established in children's homes.

Knowledge Check

1. Explain what is meant by 'institutionalisation'. *(2 marks)*
2. Describe the procedure **and** findings of **one** Romanian orphan study. *(6 marks)*
3. Describe what research has shown about the effects of institutionalisation. *(6 marks)*
4. Discuss research into the effects of institutionalisation. *(12 marks AS, 16 marks AL)*

Influence of early attachment on later relationships

Spec spotlight

The influence of early attachment on childhood and adult relationships, including the role of an internal working model.

Children who have positive early relationships tend to have successful relationships in later life. Go on then you two – that's probably worth an awkward high five.

Internal working models are discussed on page 58.

Apply it

All of his life Josh has had trouble forming happy relationships. As a child, he was highly upset whenever his mum left the room, but didn't want to know her when she came back. At school, he bullied other children, typically those he considered weaker than himself. As an adult, Josh has always found it difficult to make friends and seems unable to maintain friendships.

Using the concept of an internal working model, explain how Josh's problems with relationships could be traced back to his infancy.

Internal working model

First attachment is a template for future relationships.	The quality of a child's first attachment is crucial because it provides a template that will affect the nature of their future relationships. This is due to the influence of the *internal working model* created by that first attachment.
Good attachment = good relationship expectations.	A child whose first experience is of a loving relationship with a reliable attachment figure assumes this is how all relationships are meant to be. They will then seek out functional relationships and behave functionally within them.
Bad attachment = bad relationship expectations.	A child with bad experiences of their first attachment will bring these experiences to bear on later relationships. This may mean they struggle to form relationships in the first place or they do not behave appropriately in them.
Childhood. Link with friendships and bullying.	Securely attached babies tend to go on to form the best quality childhood friendships (Kerns 1994). Securely attached children are less likely to be involved in bullying whereas insecure–avoidant children are most likely to be victims and insecure–resistant are most likely to be bullies (Myron-Wilson and Smith 1998).
Adulthood. Link with parenting style and romantic relationships.	People base their parenting style on their internal working model. Bailey *et al.* (2007) found the majority of mothers had the same attachment classification to their babies as they had to their own mothers. Hazan and Shaver (below) found a link between attachment type and quality of adult romantic relationships.

Hazan and Shaver (1987) The love quiz

PROCEDURE	The researchers analysed 620 replies to a 'love quiz' printed in an American local newspaper.
	The quiz assessed three different aspects of relationships: (1) current and most important relationship, (2) general love experiences, (3) attachment type.
FINDINGS AND CONCLUSIONS	The respondents' attachment type was reflected in their romantic relationships: • *Secure respondents* were the most likely to have good and longer-lasting romantic relationships. • *Avoidant respondents* tended to be jealous and fear intimacy.

One strength is strong research support.

There are many studies showing a link between infant attachment type and later development, including bullying, success in romantic relationships and parenting.

A review by Fearon and Roisman (2017) concluded that infant attachment influenced development in many ways. Disorganised attachment was most predictive e.g. of later mental disorder.

This means that insecure attachment appears to convey a disadvantage for children's development.

Counterpoint

Not all evidence supports the link between infant attachment and later development. For example the Regensburg longitudinal study (Becker-Stoll et al. 2008) found no evidence of continuity of attachment type from age 1 to 16 years.

This means it is not clear how strongly attachment influences later development.

One limitation is validity issues with retrospective studies.

Most studies assess participants' attachment type in adulthood (not in infancy) using questionnaires or interviews. These rely on honest answers.

A further problem is that these studies assess attachment in late childhood or adulthood and assume that it has remained the same since infancy.

This means that the measures of attachment may not be **valid**.

Another limitation is possible confounding variables.

Some studies do make assessments of infant attachment and follow up children, assessing their later development.

However, these studies may be affected by confounding variables. For example parenting style and personality might affect both attachment and later development.

This means that we can never be entirely sure that it is infant attachment and not some other factor that is influencing later development.

Evaluation extra: Balancing opportunity and risk.

Knowing that insecure infant attachment leads to increased risk of later developmental problems can provide opportunities to intervene.

However this may lead to overly pessimistic expectations and create a self-fulfilling prophecy.

This means that knowing someone's attachment status may do more harm than good.

Baby–parent attachment may be assessed retrospectively using questionnaires – but responses may not always be truthful.

Knowledge Check

1. Explain what is meant by the 'internal working model'.
   (2 marks)

2. Outline what research has shown concerning the influence of early attachments on later relationships. Refer to the internal working model in your answer. *(6 marks)*

3. Explain **one** limitation of research on the influence of early attachments on later relationships. *(4 marks)*

4. Discuss research into the influence of early attachments on both childhood **and** adult relationships.
   (12 marks AS, 16 marks AL)

Origins of Psychology

Spec spotlight

Origins of Psychology: Wundt, introspection and the emergence of Psychology as a science.

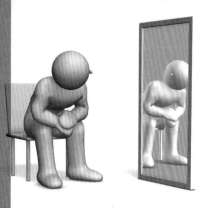

If you're not sure what is meant by 'introspection', you need to take a long hard look at yourself.

Science is defined as a means of acquiring knowledge through *systematic and objective* investigation. The aim is to discover general laws. Experiments are the ideal of science but not the only scientific method used by psychologists.

Apply it

Two students are discussing whether or not psychology can really be considered a science. Tara thinks it can and argues that Wundt made a significant contribution to the development of Psychology as a science. Max accepts that behaviourism is quite scientific but reckons that many approaches in psychology are not scientific at all.

Can psychology be regarded as a science? Explain your answer, referring to Tara's and Max's views.

Wundt and introspection

Wilhelm Wundt established the first psychology lab.	Opened in Leipzig, Germany in 1879. The aim was to describe the nature of human consciousness (the 'mind') in a carefully controlled and scientific environment – a lab.
Introspection.	Wundt pioneered introspection, the first systematic experimental attempt to study the mind.
Controlled procedures.	The same **standardised** instructions were given to all participants and stimuli (objects or sounds) were presented in the same order (standardised procedures). For instance, participants were given a ticking metronome and they would report their thoughts, images and sensations, which were then recorded.
Structuralism.	Introspection led to identifying the structure of consciousness by breaking it up into the basic structures: thoughts, images and sensations. This marked the beginning of scientific psychology, separating it from its broader philosophical roots.

Emergence of Psychology as a science

1900s Early behaviourists rejected introspection.	Watson (1913) argued that introspection was subjective, in that it is influenced by a personal perspective. According to the **behaviourist** approach, 'scientific' psychology should only study phenomena that can be observed and measured.
1930s Behaviourist scientific approach dominated psychology.	Skinner (1953) brought the language and rigour of the natural sciences into psychology. The behaviourists' focus on learning, and the use of carefully controlled lab studies, would dominate psychology for 50 years.
1950s Cognitive approach studied mental processes scientifically.	Following the computer revolution of the 1950s, the study of mental processes was seen as legitimate within psychology. **Cognitive** psychologists likened the mind to a computer and tested their predictions about memory and attention using experiments.
1980s The biological approach introduced technological advances.	**Biological** psychologists have taken advantage of recent advances in technology, including recording brain activity, using scanning techniques such as **fMRI** and **EEG**, and advanced genetic research.

One strength is that aspects of Wundt's work are scientific.

For instance, he recorded the introspections within a controlled lab environment.

He also standardised his procedures so that all participants received the same information and were tested in the same way.

Therefore Wundt's research can be considered a forerunner to the later scientific approaches in psychology that were to come.

One limitation is that other aspects of Wundt's research are subjective.

Wundt relied on participants self-reporting their 'private' mental processes. Such data is subjective. Participants may also have hidden some of their thoughts.

This makes it difficult to establish meaningful 'laws of behaviour', one of the aims of science.

Therefore Wundt's early efforts to study the mind were naïve and would not meet the criteria of scientific enquiry.

Evaluation extra: Wundt's contribution.

Wundt produced the first academic journal for psychological research and wrote the first textbook. He is often referred to as the 'father' of modern psychology.

His pioneering research set the foundation for approaches that were to come, particularly the behaviourist approach and cognitive psychology.

This shows that, despite the flaws in his early experimental research, Wundt made a significant contribution to psychology.

One strength is that research in modern psychology can claim to be scientific.

Psychology has the same aims as the natural sciences – to describe, understand, predict and control behaviour.

Learning, cognitive and biological approaches all use scientific methods e.g. lab studies are controlled and unbiased.

Throughout the 20th century and beyond, psychology has established itself as a scientific discipline.

One limitation of psychology is that some approaches use subjective data.

Humanistic approach does not formulate general laws of behaviour. **Psychodynamic** approach uses case studies with unrepresentative samples.

Psychologists study humans who are active participants and therefore respond to **demand characteristics**.

Therefore a scientific approach to the study of human thought and experience is not desirable or possible.

Evaluation extra: Paradigm.

Kuhn said that any science must have a paradigm: a set of principles, assumptions and methods that all people who work within that subject agree on.

Psychology does not have a paradigm. However, most would agree it is the study of mind and behaviour.

This suggests that the question of whether psychology is a science remains unanswered.

Do you agree with this conclusion?

Revision BOOSTER

An essay on Wundt's work alone is perhaps less likely than other areas in the Approaches section. One possibility is that you might be asked to 'outline and briefly evaluate the work of Wundt' or 'briefly discuss the contribution of Wundt to the emergence of Psychology as a science'. In both of these questions evaluative points would be required so these are included here.

Similarly, it is debatable whether an essay would be set on the *emergence of Psychology as a science*, but for evaluation, you could consider which approaches in psychology would meet scientific criteria and which would not.

I ♥ PSYCHOLOGY

Yes of course you do – but the question of whether Psychology is a science is not one that has a straightforward answer...

Download suggested answers to the Knowledge Check questions from tinyurl.com/y8kjyvwe

Knowledge Check

1. Explain what Wundt meant by 'introspection'. *(2 marks)*
2. Outline **and** briefly evaluate the work of Wundt. *(8 marks)*
3. Briefly discuss the emergence of Psychology as a science. *(6 marks)*

Learning approaches: The behaviourist approach

Spec spotlight

Learning approaches:
i) The behaviourist approach, including classical conditioning and Pavlov's research, operant conditioning, types of reinforcement and Skinner's research.

'Conditioning' means 'learning'.

'Have you heard of a bloke called Ivan Pavlov?'

'I must admit, the name rings a bell.'

Apply it

Joel is addicted to online fruit machine gambling. He spends a lot of time and money on this and other forms of online gambling.

1. Explain Joel's gambling addiction in terms of operant conditioning. Use the concepts of positive and negative reinforcement in your explanation.

2. Explain a feature of operant conditioning that might lead to a reduction in his gambling behaviour.

Rat presses lever in Skinner box and receives food – positive reinforcement for the lever-pressing behaviour.

Key features of the behaviourist approach

Focus on observable behaviour only.	The **behaviourist** approach is only concerned with studying behaviour that can be observed and measured. It is not concerned with mental processes of the mind. *Introspection* was rejected by behaviourists as its concepts were vague and difficult to measure.
Controlled lab studies.	Behaviourists tried to maintain more control and objectivity within their research and relied on lab studies to achieve this.
Use of non-human animals.	Behaviourists suggest the processes that govern learning are the same in all species, so animals (e.g. rats, cats, dogs and pigeons) can replace humans as experimental subjects.

Classical conditioning *Pavlov's research.*	**Classical conditioning** refers to learning by association.	**Pavlov's research** – conditioning dogs to salivate when a bell rings:
		Before conditioning:
	UCS $\rightarrow$ UCR NS $\rightarrow$ no response	**UCS** = food, **UCR** = salivation, **NS** = bell
		During conditioning:
	NS + UCS	Bell and food occur at same time.
		After conditioning:
	CS $\rightarrow$ CR	**CS** = bell, **CR** = salivation
		Pavlov showed how a neutral stimulus (bell) can come to elicit a new learned response (**conditioned response**, CR) through association.
	(See examples on pages 56 and 96.)	

Operant conditioning *Skinner's research.*	**Operant conditioning** refers to learning as an active process whereby humans and animals *operate* on their environment. Behaviour is shaped and maintained by its *consequences.*	**Skinner's research** – rats and pigeons, in specially designed cages (Skinner boxes). When a rat activated a lever (or a pigeon pecked a disc) it was *rewarded* with a food pellet. A desirable consequence led to behaviour being repeated. If pressing a lever meant an animal avoided an electric shock, the behaviour would also be repeated.

Three types of consequences of behaviour.	**Positive reinforcement** – receiving a reward when behaviour is performed. **Negative reinforcement** – avoiding something unpleasant when a behaviour is performed. **Punishment** – an unpleasant consequence of behaviour. Positive reinforcement and negative reinforcement increase the likelihood that behaviour will be repeated. Punishment decreases it.

One strength of behaviourism is that it uses well-controlled research.

The approach has focused on the careful measurement of observable behaviour within controlled lab settings.

Behaviourists have broken behaviour down into stimulus–response units and studied causal relationships.

This suggests that behaviourist experiments have scientific credibility.

Counterpoint

However this approach may oversimplify learning and ignore important influences on behaviour (e.g. thought). Other approaches (e.g. **social learning** and **cognitive**) incorporate mental processes.

This suggests learning is more complex than just what we can observe.

One strength is behaviourist laws of learning have real-world application.

The principles of conditioning have been applied to a broad range of real-world behaviours and problems.

Token economy systems reward appropriate behaviour with tokens that are exchanged for privileges (operant conditioning). Successfully used in prisons and psychiatric wards.

This increases the value of the behaviourist approach because it has widespread application.

One limitation is behaviourism is a form of environmental **determinism**.

The approach sees all behaviour as determined by past experiences that have been conditioned and ignores any influence that **free will** may have on behaviour.

Skinner suggested that free will was an illusion. When something happens we may think 'I made the decision to do that' but our past conditioning determined the outcome.

This is an extreme position and ignores the influence of conscious decision-making processes on behaviour (as suggested by the cognitive approach).

Evaluation extra: Ethical issues.

Procedures such as the Skinner box allowed behaviourists to maintain a high degree of control over their experimental 'subjects'.

However the animals were housed in harsh, cramped conditions and deliberately kept below their natural weight so they were always hungry.

Therefore there is a question of benefits versus costs – some would argue that there have been enormous benefits (e.g. application to therapy) which offsets the harm the animals experienced.

Revision BOOSTER

When writing critical points it is desirable to explain them thoroughly.

- Always start with a statement of your point (P).
- Provide further explanation (E) using examples (E) and/or evidence (E).
- If you can, end your evaluation with a T statement (This shows that..., Therefore ...).

CRAIG SWANSON © WWW.PERSPICUITY.COM

A former participant in the Skinner box studies struggles to find work.

Knowledge Check

1. Explain what is meant by 'classical conditioning'.
   (2 marks)

2. Outline Skinner's research into operant conditioning.
   (4 marks)

3. Explain how **two** types of reinforcement could be used by a parent to encourage their child to come home by 9pm on a school night.
   (4 marks)

4. Discuss the behaviourist approach. Refer to the research of both Pavlov **and** Skinner in your answer.
   (12 marks AS, 16 marks AL)

Learning approaches: Social learning theory

Spec spotlight

Learning approaches: ii) Social learning theory including imitation, identification, modelling, vicarious reinforcement, the role of mediational processes and Bandura's research.

Imitation – the sincerest form of flattery apparently.

Apply it

Barney is an eight-year-old boy. He's noticed one of the older boys in his primary school bossing younger children around. This older boy is physically aggressive, sometimes to get money or sweets, or just to show everyone who's boss.

1. Explain the social learning processes which may lead to Barney becoming aggressive to the younger children himself. Refer in your explanation to the roles of imitation, identification, modelling and vicarious reinforcement.

2. In terms of mediational processes, explain **three** ways in which Barney is unlikely to become aggressive and bossy.

Note that modelling is a named term on the specification that can be used in two subtly different ways. From the observer's perspective, 'modelling' is imitating the behaviour of a role model. From the role model's perspective, it is demonstrating behaviour that may be imitated.

Key features of social learning theory (SLT)

Learning that occurs indirectly.	Albert Bandura agreed with the **behaviourist** approach that learning occurs through experience.
	However, he also proposed that learning takes place in a social context through *observation* and *imitation* of others' behaviour.
Learning related to consequences of behaviour – *vicarious reinforcement*.	Children (and adults) observe other people's behaviour and take note of its consequences. Behaviour that is seen to be rewarded (reinforced) is more likely to be copied = vicarious reinforcement.
Mediational (cognitive) processes play a crucial role in learning.	There are four mediational processes in learning: 1. *Attention* – whether behaviour is noticed. 2. *Retention* – whether behaviour is remembered. 3. *Motor reproduction* – being able to do it. 4. *Motivation* – the will to perform the behaviour. The first two relate to the learning, the last two to the performance (so, unlike behaviourism, learning and performance do not have to occur together).
Identification with role models is important.	People are more likely to imitate the behaviour of those with whom they identify. Such role models are similar to the observer, attractive and have high status.

Bandura's research

	Bandura *et al.* (1961)	**Bandura and Walters (1963)**
PROCEDURES	Children watched either: • An adult behaving aggressively towards a Bobo doll. • An adult behaving non-aggressively towards a Bobo doll.	Children saw adult who was: • Rewarded. • Punished. • There was no consequence.
FINDINGS AND CONCLUSIONS	When given their own doll to play with, the children who had seen aggression were much more aggressive towards the doll.	When given their own doll, the children who saw the aggression *rewarded* were much more aggressive themselves.

The Bobo doll studies suggest that children are likely to imitate (model) acts of violence if they observe these in an adult role model.

It is also the case that **modelling** aggressive behaviour is more likely if such behaviour is seen to be rewarded (vicarious reinforcement).

One strength is SLT emphasises the importance of cognitive factors.

Neither **classical conditioning** nor **operant conditioning** can offer a comprehensive account of human learning on their own because cognitive factors are omitted.

Humans and animals store information about the behaviour of others and use this to make judgements about when it is appropriate to perform certain actions.

This shows that SLT provides a more complete explanation of human learning than the behaviourist approach by recognising the role of mediational processes.

Counterpoint

Recent research suggests that observational learning is controlled by mirror neurons in the brain, which allow us to empathise with and imitate other people.

This suggests that SLT may make too little reference to the influence of biological factors on social learning.

One limitation is SLT relies too heavily on evidence from contrived lab studies.

Many of Bandura's ideas were developed through observation of children's behaviour in lab settings and this raises the problem of **demand characteristics**.

The main purpose of a Bobo doll is to hit it. So the children in those studies may have been behaving as they thought was expected.

Thus the research may tell us little about how children actually learn aggression in everyday life.

Another strength is SLT has real-world application.

Social learning principles can account for how children learn from other people around them, as well as through the media, and this can explain how cultural norms are transmitted.

This has proved useful in understanding a range of behaviours such as how children come to understand their gender role by imitating role models in the media.

This increases the value of SLT as it can account for real-world behaviour.

Evaluation extra: Reciprocal determinism.

Bandura emphasised *reciprocal determinism* – we are influenced by our environment, but we also exert an influence upon it through the behaviours we choose to perform.

This element of choice suggests there is some **free will** in the way we behave.

This is a more realistic and flexible position than is suggested by the behaviourist approach as it recognises the role we play in shaping our own environment.

Revision BOOSTER

Evaluation points like these do not just come in handy for longer essay-style questions. It is possible you might be asked for a single strength or limitation as part of a short-answer question. Also, some questions ask for a 'brief discussion' of particular approaches. For such questions, our counterpoints would do the job nicely.

The word 'bobo' is Spanish for 'clown'. The word 'doll' is English for 'doll'.

The specification for this topic includes the terms: imitation, identification, modelling, vicarious reinforcement, the role of mediational processes and Bandura's research.

This means that exam questions may include any of these.

Knowledge Check

1. Explain what is meant by 'identification' in social learning theory. *(2 marks)*

2. Outline Bandura's research into social learning. *(4 marks)*

3. With reference to mediational processes in social learning, explain how a child might learn to bake a cake by watching his mother. *(6 marks)*

4. Describe **and** evaluate the social learning approach. *(12 marks AS, 16 marks AL)*

The cognitive approach

Spec spotlight

The cognitive approach: the study of internal mental processes, the role of schema, the use of theoretical and computer models to explain and make inferences about mental processes. The emergence of cognitive neuroscience.

Revision BOOSTER

Note the difference between a theoretical model and a computer model. Both are named on the specification so you need to be able to provide an explanation and an example of each.

Also note the other terms that you can be examined on: internal mental processes, schema, inferences and the emergence of cognitive neuroscience.

**PARIS
IN THE
THE SPRING**

Did you spot the second 'the'? If not, that'll be your schema then.

Key features of the cognitive approach

Scientific study of mental processes.	In direct contrast to the **behaviourist** approach, the **cognitive** approach argues that mental processes should be studied, e.g. studying perception and memory.
Role of *inference* in the study of mental processes.	Mental processes are 'private' and cannot be observed, so cognitive psychologists study them indirectly by making inferences (assumptions) about what is going on inside people's heads on the basis of their behaviour.
The idea of *schema* is central to the cognitive approach.	• Schema are packages of information developed through experience. • They act as a 'mental framework' for the interpretation of incoming information received by the cognitive system. • Babies are born with simple motor schema for innate behaviours such as sucking and grasping. • As we get older, our schema become more detailed and sophisticated.
Theoretical models to explain mental processes.	The information processing approach suggests that information flows through a sequence of stages that include input, storage and retrieval, as in the *multi-store model* (see page 32).
Computer models to explain mental processes.	Computer models refer to programmes that can be run on a computer to imitate the human mind (e.g. conversational machines to deal with consumer enquiries). By running such a programme psychologists can test their ideas about information processing.
The emergence of *cognitive neuroscience*.	• Cognitive neuroscience is the scientific study of the influence of brain structures *(neuro)* on mental processes *(cognition)*. • With advances in brain scanning technology in the last twenty years, scientists have been able to describe the neurological basis of mental processing. • This includes research in memory that has linked *episodic* and *semantic memories* to opposite sides of the **prefrontal cortex** in the brain (Tulving *et al.* 1994). • Scanning techniques have also proved useful in establishing the neurological basis of some disorders, e.g. the *parahippocampal gyrus* and OCD.

One strength is the cognitive approach uses scientific and objective methods.

Cognitive psychologists have always employed controlled and rigorous methods of study, e.g. lab studies, in order to infer cognitive processes at work.

In addition the two fields of biology and cognitive psychology come together (cognitive neuroscience) to enhance the scientific basis of study.

This means that the study of the mind has established a credible, scientific basis.

Counterpoint

The use of inference means cognitive psychology can occasionally be too abstract and theoretical. Also, research often uses artificial stimuli (such as word lists).

Therefore, research on cognitive processes may lack **external validity** and not represent everyday experience.

Probably why they call it 'cog psychology'.

Another strength of the approach is the application to everyday life.

The cognitive approach is dominant in psychology today and has been applied to a wide range of practical and theoretical contexts.

For instance, *artificial intelligence* (AI) and the development of robots, the treatment of depression and improving eyewitness testimony.

This supports the value of the cognitive approach.

Apply it

Amber is two years old. Her parents have noticed that her play behaviour is not random, but seems to demonstrate certain patterns. For example, she is obsessed with Russian dolls and loves to get adults to remove each doll one at a time, then replace them over and over again. She really enjoys putting smaller objects inside larger ones and making dens and sitting in them.

Explain how the concept of a schema can help us understand such patterns of play.

One limitation is that the approach is based on machine reductionism.

Although there are similarities between the operations of the human mind and computers (inputs-outputs, central processor, storage systems), the computer analogy has been criticised.

For instance, emotion and motivation have been shown to influence accuracy of recall, e.g. in eyewitness accounts. These factors are not considered within the computer analogy.

This suggests that machine reductionism may weaken the validity of the cognitive approach.

Not everyone agrees with this conclusion. What do you think?

Evaluation extra: Soft determinism.

The cognitive approach recognises that our cognitive system operates within certain limits, but we are free to make decisions before responding to a stimulus (**soft determinism**).

This is in contrast to the behaviourist approach which suggests we are passive to the environment and lack free choice in our behaviour.

This suggests that the cognitive approach takes a more flexible middle-ground position and is more in line with our subjective sense of **free will**.

Knowledge Check

1. Outline what cognitive psychologists mean by 'schema'. *(3 marks)*
2. Briefly explain how theoretical models are used in cognitive psychology to make inferences about mental processes. *(4 marks)*
3. Outline the emergence of cognitive neuroscience in psychology. *(6 marks)*
4. Discuss the cognitive approach. *(8 marks)*
5. Describe **and** evaluate the cognitive approach. *(12 marks AS, 16 marks AL)*

The biological approach

Spec spotlight

The biological approach: the influence of genes, biological structures and neurochemistry on behaviour. Genotype and phenotype, genetic basis of behaviour, evolution and behaviour.

Yeah they look cute now but wait until they wake up.

Apply it

Wilson's disease is a rare genetic disorder which can affect several of the body's systems, including the brain. This results in symptoms such as clumsiness, speech problems, difficulty in concentrating, depression and anxiety. It is caused by the body storing too much copper, a mineral which we need in just tiny amounts. There is no cure. But the disorder can be managed by reducing the amount of copper in the person's diet, and carefully monitoring blood and urine, so the individual can develop normally.

Using Wilson's disease as an example, explain the difference between genotype and phenotype.

Key features of the biological approach

Everything psychological is at first biological.	If we want to fully understand human behaviour we must look to biological structures and processes within the body, such as *genes* and *neurochemistry*.
The mind and body are one and the same.	From the **biological** approach, the mind lives in the brain – meaning that all thoughts, feelings and behaviour ultimately have a physical basis. This is in contrast to the **cognitive** approach which sees the mind as separate from the brain.
Neurochemical basis of behaviour.	Neurochemistry refers to the action of chemicals in the brain – neurotransmitters transmit messages. An imbalance of neurotransmitters may be a cause of some mental disorders, e.g. underproduction of **serotonin** in OCD.
Genetic basis of behaviour.	Psychological characteristics (e.g. intelligence) are inherited. Twin studies are used to investigate genetic influences. Concordance rates between twins are calculated – the extent to which twins share the same characteristic. Higher concordance rates among identical (monozygotic, MZ) twins (genetically 100% the same) than non-identical (dizygotic, DZ) twins (about 50% the same) is evidence of a genetic basis.
The difference between *genotype* and *phenotype*.	• A person's genotype is their actual genetic make-up. • Phenotype is the way that genes are expressed through physical, behavioural and psychological characteristics. • The expression of genotype (phenotype) is influenced by environmental factors. • For example, *phenylketonuria (PKU)* is a genetic disorder that can be prevented by a restricted diet. • This suggests that much of human behaviour depends on the interaction of nature and nurture.
Theory of evolution is used by the biological approach to explain behaviour.	• Darwin (1859) proposed the theory of natural selection. • Any genetically determined behaviour that enhances survival *and* reproduction will be passed on to future generations. • Such genes are described as *adaptive* and give the possessor and their offspring advantages. • For instance, attachment behaviours in newborns promote survival and are therefore adaptive and naturally selected.

One strength of the biological approach is its real-world application.

Understanding of neurochemical processes in the brain has led to the use of psychoactive drugs to treat serious mental disorders.

For example, drugs that treat clinical depression increase levels of the neurotransmitter serotonin at the synapse and reduce depressive symptoms.

This means that people with depression are able to manage their condition and live a relatively normal life, rather than being confined to hospital.

Counterpoint

However, antidepressant drugs do not work for everyone. Cipriani *et al.* (2018) compared 21 antidepressant drugs and found wide variations in their effectiveness.

This challenges the value of the biological approach as it suggests that brain chemistry alone may not account for all cases of depression.

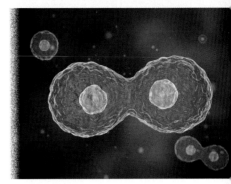

Biology is the only science in which multiplication is the same thing as division.

Another strength is the biological approach uses scientific methods.

In order to investigate both genetic and neurochemical factors, the biological approach makes use of a range of precise and objective methods.

These include scanning techniques (e.g. **fMRI**), which assess biological processes in ways that are not open to bias.

This means that the biological approach is based on objective and reliable data.

Biological psychologists believe that behaviours have evolved because they provide some advantage, in terms of allowing us to adapt to our environments. Examples from this book include: (1) conforming to the behaviour of other members of a group, (2) having both short-term and long-term memories, (3) experiencing OCD (which many psychologists believe has a genetic basis).

For each of these examples, explain what the adaptive advantages could be.

One limitation is that biological explanations are determinist.

Biological explanations tend to be determinist in that they see human behaviour as governed by internal, genetic causes over which we have no control.

However, the way genotype is expressed (phenotype) is heavily influenced by the environment. Not even genetically identical twins look and think exactly the same.

This suggests that the biological view is too simplistic and ignores the mediating effects of the environment.

Evaluation extra: Natural selection.

Critics of Darwin's work, such as Popper, claim it is not possible to show evolution happening, only that it has taken place (unfalsifiable).

However, others argue that natural selection is supported by fossil records (e.g. gradually changing forms from dinosaurs to birds).

This suggests that although natural selection is not able to tell us what species will evolve into, it provides an adequate account of past development.

Knowledge Check

1. Outline **two** key features of the biological approach in psychology. *(6 marks)*

2. Explain the difference between genotype and phenotype. *(4 marks)*

3. Explain the process of evolution. Include an example in your answer. *(4 marks)*

4. Describe **and** evaluate the biological approach in psychology. *(12 marks AS, 16 marks AL)*

Biopsychology: The nervous system

Spec spotlight

The divisions of the nervous system: central and peripheral (somatic and autonomic).

The function of the endocrine system: glands and hormones.

The fight or flight response including the role of adrenaline.

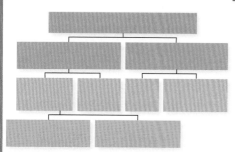

You might have to label a diagram in the exam. Nervous..?

The nervous system acts more rapidly than the endocrine system but they are both very fast. The nervous system's average response time is 0.25 seconds but may be as quick as 100 milliseconds. The endocrine responses are slower because hormones have to travel through the bloodstream (about 2 or 3 seconds) but last longer.

Apply it

Leah is being interviewed for a job. It's really important to her and everything is going fine, until one interviewer asks her a question and she suddenly realises she doesn't know the answer. She tries hard to remember the information she needs but can't concentrate. She can hear her heart beating faster, her face is reddening, her hands are shaking and she feels sick.

Explain the roles of (1) the CNS, (2) the ANS, and (3) the endocrine system in Leah's behaviour.

The nervous system

The key features of the *nervous system*.	The nervous system is a specialised network of cells and our primary communication system. It is based on electrical (and chemical) signals whereas the endocrine system (facing page) is based on hormones.

The nervous system has two main functions:

1. To collect, process and respond to information in the environment;
2. To co-ordinate the working of different organs and cells in the body.

The structure and function of the *central nervous system* (CNS).	• CNS is made up of the brain and the spinal cord.

- The brain is the centre of conscious awareness.
- The outer layer of the brain, the cerebral cortex (3 mm thick), is highly developed in humans and is what distinguishes our higher mental functions from those of animals.
- The brain is divided into two hemispheres.

- The spinal cord is an extension of the brain and is responsible for reflex actions.
- It passes messages to and from the brain and connects nerves to the PNS.

The structure and function of the *peripheral nervous system* (PNS).	• The PNS transmits messages, via millions of neurons, to and from the nervous system.

- The PNS is further subdivided into:
  - *Autonomic nervous system* (ANS) governs vital functions in the body such as breathing, heart rate, digestion, sexual arousal and stress responses.
  - *Somatic nervous system* (SNS) governs muscle movement and receives information from sensory receptors.

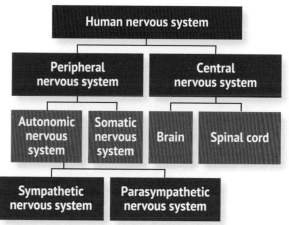

The major subdivisions of the human nervous system.

The endocrine system

The key features of the *endocrine system*.	The endocrine system works alongside the nervous system to control vital functions in the body through the action of hormones. It works more slowly than the nervous system (seconds instead of milliseconds) but has widespread and powerful effects.
Glands.	Glands are organs in the body that produce hormones. The key endocrine gland is the *pituitary gland*, located in the brain. It is called the 'master gland' because it controls the release of hormones from all the other endocrine glands in the body.
Hormones.	Hormones are secreted in the bloodstream and affect any cell in the body that has a receptor for that particular hormone. For example, *thyroxine* produced by the thyroid gland affects cells in the heart and also cells throughout the body which increase metabolic rates. This in turn affects growth rates.
The endocrine system and the ANS work together. For example, the *fight or flight response*.	Often the endocrine system and the ANS work in parallel, for instance during a *stressful event*. • Stressor perceived by *hypothalamus* which activates the *pituitary*. • The *sympathetic nervous system* is now aroused. • *Adrenaline* (the stress hormone) is released from the *adrenal medulla* into the bloodstream. This delivers the aroused state causing changes in target organs in the body e.g. increased heart rate, dilation of pupils, decreased production of saliva. This is called the fight or flight response. • Immediate and automatic – this response happens the instant a threat is perceived. • *Parasympathetic nervous system* (rest and digest) takes over once the threat has passed. This returns the body to its resting state. This acts as a 'brake' and reduces the activities of the body that were increased by the actions of the sympathetic branch (rest and digest).

© Mike Baldwin / Cornered

Revision BOOSTER

Questions in this section are likely to be either descriptive or application. There is very little scope for evaluation/discussion in this section so an essay in biopsychology is very unlikely.

Sympathetic state	Parasympathetic state
Increases heart rate	Decreases heart rate
Increases breathing rate	Decreases breathing rate
Dilates pupils	Constricts pupils
Inhibits digestion	Stimulates digestion
Inhibits saliva production	Stimulates saliva production
Contracts rectum	Relaxes rectum

Knowledge Check

1. Using an example, explain what is meant by the 'fight or flight response'. *(4 marks)*
2. Identify **and** outline **two** divisions of the peripheral nervous system. *(4 marks)*
3. Describe **two** glands of the endocrine system. *(4 marks)*
4. Explain the difference between the nervous system **and** the endocrine system. *(4 marks)*

Biopsychology: Neurons

Spec spotlight

The structure and function of sensory, relay and motor neurons.

The process of synaptic transmission including reference to neurotransmitters, excitation and inhibition.

CNS = central nervous system.

PNS = peripheral nervous system.

The structure and function of neurons

Types of *neurons*.

There are 100 billion nerve cells (neurons) in the human nervous system, 80% of which are located in the brain.

By transmitting signals *electrically* and *chemically*, these provide the nervous system with its primary means of communication.

There are three types of neuron:

1. *Sensory neurons* carry messages from the PNS to the CNS. They have long dendrites and short axons. Located in the PNS in clusters called ganglias.
2. *Relay neurons* connect sensory neurons to motor or other relay neurons. They have short dendrites and short axons. Of all neurons, 97% are relay neurons and most are in the brain and visual system.
3. *Motor neurons* connect the CNS to effectors such as muscles and glands. They have short dendrites and long axons. Cell bodies may be in the CNS but long axons form part of PNS.

The structure of a neuron.

Neurons vary in size but all share the same basic structure:

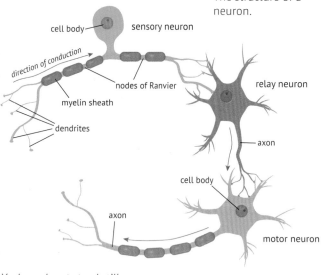

- *Cell body* (or soma) – includes a nucleus which contains the genetic material of the cell.

- *Dendrites* – branchlike structures that protrude from the cell body. These carry nerve impulses from neighbouring neurons towards the cell body.

- *Axon* – carries the electrical impulse away from the cell body down the length of the neuron.

  o It is covered in a fatty layer of *myelin sheath* that protects the axon.

  o Gaps in the axon called *nodes of Ranvier* speed up the transmission of the impulse.

- *Terminal buttons* at the end of the axon communicate with the next neuron in the chain across a gap called the *synapse*.

Yeah, my heart stood still, a neuron ron yeah a neuron ron.

Ask your parents...

Revision BOOSTER

It is important that you can describe the structure and function of each of the three types of neuron as these are specifically named on the specification.

Electrical transmission. The firing of a neuron.

When a neuron is in a resting state the inside of the cell is *negatively charged* compared to the outside.

When a neuron is activated, the inside of the cell becomes *positively charged* for a split second causing an *action potential* to occur.

This creates an electrical impulse that travels down the axon towards the end of the neuron.

Synaptic transmission

A *synapse*.	Each neuron is separated from the next by an extremely tiny gap called the synapse.
Chemical transmission. The events that occur at the synapse.	Signals within neurons are transmitted electrically, but signals between neurons are transmitted chemically across the synapse. When the electrical impulse reaches the end of the neuron (the *presynaptic terminal*) it triggers the release of *neurotransmitter* from tiny sacs called *synaptic vesicles*. Once a neurotransmitter crosses the gap, it is taken up by a *postsynaptic receptor site* on the next neuron, so the impulse only ever travels in one direction. The chemical message is converted back into an electrical impulse and the process of electrical transmission begins.
Neurotransmitters.	Neurotransmitters are chemicals that diffuse across the synapse to the next neuron in the chain. Many neurotransmitters have been identified. Each has its own specific molecular structure that fits perfectly into a postsynaptic receptor site, like a lock and key. Each has specific functions. For example: • *Acetylcholine* (ACh) found where a motor neuron meets a muscle, causing muscles to contract. • **Serotonin** affects mood and social behaviour (among other things) which is why it has been implicated as a cause of depression.
Excitation and inhibition.	Neurotransmitters generally have either an excitatory or inhibitory effect on the neighbouring neuron. • *Adrenaline* – generally excitatory, increasing the positive charge of the postsynaptic neuron, making it more likely the postsynaptic neuron will fire. • *Serotonin* – generally inhibitory, increasing the negative charge of the postsynaptic neuron, making it less likely the postsynaptic neuron will fire. • **Dopamine** is an unusual neurotransmitter as it is equally likely to have excitatory or inhibitory effects on the postsynaptic neuron.
Summation.	Excitatory and inhibitory influences are summed and must reach a certain threshold in order for the action potential of the postsynaptic neuron to be triggered. If the net effect of the neurotransmitters is inhibitory then the postsynaptic neuron is less likely to fire (i.e. no electrical signal is transmitted). It is more likely to fire if the net effect is excitatory.

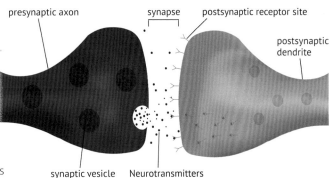

presynaptic axon   synapse   postsynaptic receptor site

postsynaptic dendrite

synaptic vesicle   Neurotransmitters in the synapse

My friend just burst into my room and asked me what an electrical synapse in the human body was.

The nerve.

Apply it

Sabiha loves chocolate. She eats it all the time and really believes that it gives her a 'boost' and makes her feel happier. Her friend Bev tells her that's probably because chocolate contains chemicals that have a real effect on the neurotransmitters of the nervous system.

Use your knowledge of synaptic transmission to explain what is happening at Sabiha's synapses.

Knowledge Check

1. Explain the difference between a motor neuron **and** a relay neuron. *(2 marks)*
2. Briefly describe the structure of a neuron. *(3 marks)*
3. Briefly outline how excitation **and** inhibition are involved in synaptic transmission. *(4 marks)*
4. Briefly explain the sequence of events that take place at the synapse. *(4 marks)*

The psychodynamic approach   A LEVEL ONLY

Spec spotlight

The psychodynamic approach: the role of the unconscious, the structure of personality, that is Id, Ego and Superego, defence mechanisms including repression, denial and displacement, psychosexual stages.

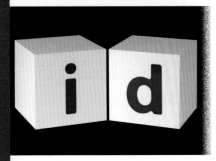

Id. A handy word to know if you're running out of tiles in Scrabble.

Revision BOOSTER

The psychodynamic approach is complex and wide-ranging. It would be easy to overdo the A01 content in an essay on this approach. Keep description of things like Freud's psychosexual stages to a minimum and only select a few examples.

Apply it

Gregory got his girlfriend's and his mum's names mixed up the other day. Felix is only interested in satisfying his own desires. Lisbeth feels guilty all the time over the smallest things. Heathcliffe's parents are having trouble getting him potty-trained. Alanis is five and wants to marry her daddy when she grows up. There are holes in Brynn's bedroom door where he punches it when he comes in from work.

Identify the psychodynamic concepts on this page that could apply to these people. Explain your choices.

Key features of the psychodynamic approach

Unconscious mind has important influence on behaviour.	Sigmund Freud suggested the mind is made up of: • Conscious – what we are aware of ('tip of the iceberg'). • Preconscious – thoughts we may become aware of through dreams and 'slips of the tongue'. • Unconscious – a vast storehouse of biological drives and instincts that influence our behaviour.
Tripartite structure of personality. Dynamic interaction between the three parts.	Freud saw personality as having three parts: • *Id* – primitive part of the personality operates on the *pleasure principle*, demands instant gratification. • *Ego* – works on the *reality principle* and is the mediator between the Id and Superego. • *Superego* – internalised sense of right and wrong, based on *morality principle*. Punishes the Ego through guilt. Appears age 5.
Five *psychosexual stages* determine adult personality.	Each stage is marked by a different conflict that the child must resolve to move on to the next. Any conflict that is unresolved leads to fixation where the child becomes 'stuck' and carries behaviours associated with that stage through to adult life.
Sequence of stages is fixed.	Oral (0–1 years) – pleasure focus = mouth, the mother's breast is the object of desire. Anal (1–3 years) – pleasure focus = anus, the child gains pleasure from withholding and eliminating faeces. Phallic (3–6 years) – pleasure focus = genital area. Latency – earlier conflicts are repressed. Genital (puberty) – sexual desires become conscious.
Oedipus complex is a *psychosexual conflict* at the phallic stage.	In the phallic stage, little boys develop incestuous feelings towards their mother and a murderous hatred for their father. Later boys repress their feelings for their mother and identify with their father, taking on his gender role and moral values. Girls of the same age experience penis envy.
Defence mechanisms used by Ego to reduce anxiety.	Unconscious strategies used by the Ego, for example: • *Repression* – forcing a distressing memory out of the conscious mind. • *Denial* – refusing to acknowledge reality. • *Displacement* – transferring feelings from their true source onto a substitute target.

One strength of the psychodynamic approach is it introduced psychotherapy.

Freud's psychoanalysis was the first attempt to treat mental disorders psychologically rather than physically.

Psychoanalysis claims to help clients deal with everyday problems by providing access to their unconscious, employing techniques such as dream analysis.

Therefore psychoanalysis is the forerunner to many modern-day 'talking therapies' (e.g. counselling).

Counterpoint

Although psychoanalysis is claimed successful for clients with mild **neuroses**, it is inappropriate, even harmful, for more serious mental disorders (such as **schizophrenia**).

Therefore Freudian therapy (and theory) may not apply to mental disorders where a client has lost touch with reality.

Another strength is the psychodynamic approach has explanatory power.

Freud's theory is controversial and often bizarre, but it has had huge influence on contemporary thought.

It has been used to explain a wide range of behaviours (moral, mental disorders) and drew attention to the influence of childhood on adult personality.

This suggests that, overall, the psychodynamic approach has had a positive influence on psychology and modern-day thinking.

One limitation is the psychodynamic approach includes untestable concepts.

Popper (philosopher of science) argued that the psychodynamic approach does not meet the scientific criterion of *falsification*, in the sense that it cannot be disproved.

Many of Freud's concepts, such as the Id or the Oedipus complex, occur at an unconscious level making them difficult, if not impossible, to test.

This means that Freud's ideas lack scientific rigour, the theory is pseudoscience ('fake' science) rather than real science.

Evaluation extra: Psychic determinism.

The psychodynamic approach suggests that much of our behaviour is determined by unconscious conflicts. Freud believed there was no such thing as an 'accident'.

However, few psychologists would accept this view as it leaves no room for **free will** beyond early childhood.

This suggests that Freud's views were too extreme as most people do have a sense of control over their behaviour.

Revision BOOSTER

Your understanding of the psychodynamic approach will be assessed at A Level only. However, you could still make comparison points between this approach and the other approaches to boost the AO3 evaluation content of an AS essay on one of the other approaches.

Freudian slip joke: Sigmund Freud walked into a bra...

Knowledge Check

1. The psychodynamic approach places emphasis on the role of unconscious in behaviour. Explain the role of the unconscious in behaviour.
   (4 marks)

2. Explain how **one** defence mechanism might help someone cope with the anxiety of losing their job.
   (2 marks)

3. Name **and** explain **one** of Freud's psychosexual stages of development. *(3 marks)*

4. Discuss the psychodynamic approach. In your answer outline **one or more** differences between the psychodynamic approach **and** the humanistic approach.
   (16 marks AL)

Humanistic psychology

Spec spotlight

Humanistic psychology: free will, self-actualisation and Maslow's hierarchy of needs, focus on the self, congruence, the role of conditions of worth. The influence on counselling psychology.

Maslow's hierarchy of needs – the lower needs must be met first, before a person can move on to the higher needs.

Self-actualisation
Self-esteem
Love and belongingness
Safety and security
Physiological needs

Apply it

Anika feels depressed because she feels that her life is empty and worthless. There were so many things she wanted to do and be but now she thinks it's just too late. She sees a person-centred therapist for counselling.

Referring to both Maslow's hierarchy of needs **and** Rogers' concept of congruence, explain how Anika could be helped to recover from depression.

Key features of the humanistic approach

Concept of *free will* is central.	**Humanistic** psychologists see humans as affected by external and internal influences but self-determining (have **free will**).
	Psychology should concern itself with subjective experience rather than general laws as we are all unique – a person-centred approach.
Hierarchy of needs has *self-actualisation* at the top.	In Maslow's hierarchy of needs the four lower levels (deficiency needs such as food, water and safety) must be met before the individual (baby, child or adult) can work towards self-actualisation – a growth need.
	Self-actualisation refers to the innate tendency that each of us has to want to achieve our full potential and become the best we can possibly be.
Focus on the self.	The *self* refers to the ideas and values that characterise 'I' and 'me' and includes perception of 'what I am' and 'what I can do'.
Aim of therapy is to establish *congruence*.	Rogers argued that personal growth requires an individual's concept of self to be congruent with their ideal self (the person they want to be).
	If too big a gap, the person will experience a state of incongruence and self-actualisation isn't possible.
Parents who impose *conditions of worth* may prevent personal growth.	Issues such as worthlessness and low self-esteem have their roots in childhood and are due to a lack of *unconditional positive regard* from our parents.
	A parent who sets boundaries on their love for their child (conditions of worth) by claiming 'I will only love you if...' is storing up psychological problems for that child in future.
Humanistic approach has had a lasting influence on *counselling psychology*.	In Rogers' client-centred therapy (counselling) an effective therapist should provide the client with three things: • Genuineness. • Empathy. • Unconditional positive regard.
	The aim is to increase feelings of self-worth and reduce incongruence between the self-concept and the ideal self.
	Rogers work transformed psychotherapy. 'Non-directive' counselling techniques are practised, not only in clinical settings, but throughout education, health, social work and industry.

One strength is that humanistic psychology is anti-reductionist.

Humanistic psychologists reject any attempt to break up behaviour and experience into smaller components.

They advocate **holism** – the idea that subjective experience can only be understood by considering the whole person (their relationships, past, present and future, etc.).

This approach may have more **validity** than its alternatives by considering meaningful human behaviour within its real-world context.

Counterpoint

However, humanistic psychology, unlike behaviourism, has relatively few concepts that can be reduced to single variables and measured.

This means that humanistic psychology in general is short on empirical evidence to support its claims.

Another strength is the approach is a positive one.

Humanistic psychologists have been praised for promoting a positive image of the human condition – seeing people as in control of their lives and having the freedom to change.

Freud saw human beings as prisoners of their past and claimed all of us existed somewhere between 'common unhappiness and absolute despair'.

Therefore humanistic psychology offers a refreshing and optimistic alternative.

One limitation is that the approach may be guilty of a cultural bias.

Many humanistic ideas (e.g. self-actualisation) would be more associated with **individualist** cultures such as the United States.

Collectivist cultures such as India, which emphasise the needs of the group, may not identify so easily with the ideals and values of humanistic psychology.

Therefore, it is possible that the approach does not apply universally and is a product of the cultural context within which it was developed.

Evaluation extra: Limited application.

Critics argue that, compared to other approaches, humanistic psychology has had limited impact within psychology, or practical application in the real world.

However, Rogerian therapy revolutionised counselling techniques and Maslow's hierarchy of needs has been used to explain motivation, particularly in the workplace.

This suggests that the approach does have value, despite the fact that (unlike other approaches) it is resolutely 'anti-scientific'.

Revision BOOSTER

In terms of the key debates in psychology, humanistic psychology often stands apart from the other approaches – it is anti-reductionist, anti-determinist and anti-science. This makes it a very useful approach for drawing comparisons with the others.

Humanistic psychologists believe we have 'free will' – a philosophical position which suggests we are able to reject internal and external influences. Not to be confused with 'Free Willy', which is a film about a whale.

Knowledge Check

1. Explain what humanistic psychologists mean by 'conditions of worth'. *(2 marks)*
2. Briefly discuss the concept of self-actualisation. *(4 marks)*
3. Briefly evaluate humanistic psychology. *(6 marks)*
4. Discuss Maslow's hierarchy of needs. Refer to self-actualisation in your answer. *(8 marks)*
5. Describe **and** evaluate the humanistic approach in psychology. *(16 marks AL)*

Comparison of approaches   A LEVEL ONLY

Spec spotlight

Comparison of approaches.

Comparing apples is somewhat easier than comparing psychological approaches....

Revision BOOSTER

The phrase 'comparison of approaches' is one that only appears on the A Level specification, not the AS. This means you cannot be explicitly asked to do this on the AS exam paper.

Having said that, comparing approaches is a good way of getting AO3 evaluation marks in an essay – as long as you make it clear how the comparison highlights a strength or limitation of the approach you have been asked about.

Apply it

This spread presents several important issues in psychology. The various approaches have unique perspectives on each one, for example nature versus nurture.

1. Which approach do you think most emphasises nature, and which most emphasises nurture? Explain how they differ.

2. Now choose **two** approaches which take a similar line on this issue (i.e. both nature or both nurture). How are they similar?

(You could answer the same questions for the other issues, such as determinism and reductionism.)

Approach	Behaviourist	Social learning	Cognitive
Views on development	The processes that underpin learning are continuous, occurring at any age.	Same as behaviourist approach.	Stage theories of child development, particularly the idea of increasingly complex schema as child gets older.
Nature versus nurture	Babies are 'blank slates' at birth. All behaviour comes about through learned associations and reinforcements.	As for behaviourist approach with additional processes of observation and imitation.	Many of our information-processing abilities and schema are innate, but are constantly refined by experience.
Reductionism	Reduces complex learning into stimulus–response units for ease of testing in a controlled lab environment.	Recognises how cognitive factors interact with the external environment.	Use of the computer analogy which ignores the role of human emotion (*machine reductionism*).
Determinism	All behaviour is environmentally determined by external forces that we cannot control, e.g. **operant conditioning** (**hard determinism**).	We are influenced by our environment and also exert some influence upon it (*reciprocal determinism*).	Suggests we are the 'choosers' of our own behaviour, but only within the limits of what we know (**soft determinism**).
Explanation and treatment of abnormal/atypical behaviour	Abnormality arises from faulty learning. Behavioural therapies aim to condition new more healthy behaviours.	Principles such as **modelling** have been used to explain (and reduce) for example aggressive behaviour.	Cognitive therapies such as cognitive behaviour therapy (CBT) used in the treatment of depression, aim to eradicate faulty thinking.

Biological	Psychodynamic	Humanistic
Genetically determined maturational changes influence behaviour, e.g. cognitive/intellectual development.	The most coherent theory of development, tying concepts and processes to age-related stages. No change after genital stage.	The development of the self is ongoing throughout life. Childhood is particularly important period e.g. parents provide **unconditional positive regard**.
Behaviour stems from the genetic blueprint we inherit from our parents (genotype), though expression of this is influenced by the environment (phenotype).	Much of our behaviour is driven by biological drives and instincts, but also a child's relationships with its parents are crucial.	Parents, friends and wider society have a critical impact on the person's self-concept.
Reduces and explains human behaviour at the level of the gene or neuron.	Reduces behaviour to the influence of biological drives, although also sees personality as a dynamic, **holistic** interaction between Id, Ego and Superego.	Anti-reductionist, based on holistic investigation of all aspects of the individual.
Much of our behaviour is directed by innate influences *(genetic determinism)*.	Unconscious forces drive our behaviour *(psychic determinism)* and these are rationalised by our conscious minds.	Human beings have **free will** and are active agents who determine their own development.
Psychoactive drugs that regulate chemical imbalances in the brain have revolutionised the treatment of mental disorders.	Anxiety disorders emerge from unconscious conflicts and overuse of defence mechanisms. Psychoanalysis aims to put people in touch with their unconscious thoughts.	Humanistic therapy, or counselling, is based on the idea that reducing incongruence will stimulate personal growth.

The TV usually does what we tell it to – but to what extent are we in control of our thoughts and behaviour?

Eclecticism

Worth noting that most modern psychologists would take an eclectic (multidisciplinary) approach to the study of human behaviour. Very few researchers work entirely within one approach.

Eclecticism refers to combining of several approaches and/or methods to provide a more comprehensive account.

For example, the **diathesis-stress model** suggests that many mental disorders are a complex interaction of genetic predisposition and environmental triggers.

Combining treatment options from several different perspectives, e.g. drugs, cognitive therapy, family therapy, has led to more effective outcomes for patients and lower relapse rates.

Knowledge Check

1. Outline **one** way in which the psychodynamic approach **and** humanistic psychology are similar. *(4 marks)*

2. Briefly discuss **one** difference between the social learning approach **and** the behaviourist approach. *(4 marks)*

3. Outline the cognitive approach. Compare the cognitive approach with the biological approach. *(16 marks AL)*

Definitions of abnormality (1)

Spec spotlight

Definitions of abnormality, including statistical infrequency and deviation from social norms.

Statistical infrequency

Defining abnormality in terms of statistics.	The most obvious way to define anything as 'normal' or 'abnormal' is in terms of the number of times it is observed.
	Statistics is about analysing numbers.
Behaviour that is rarely seen is abnormal.	Any relatively 'usual', or often seen, behaviour can be thought of as 'normal'.
	Any behaviour that is different, or rare, is 'abnormal', i.e. a statistical infrequency.
Example: IQ and *intellectual disability disorder.*	IQ is *normally distributed* (see left).
	The average IQ is 100. Most people have an IQ between 85 and 115, only 2% have a score below 70.
	Those individuals scoring below 70 are statistically unusual or 'abnormal' and are diagnosed with intellectual disability disorder.

Graph showing a normal distribution of IQ in the population.

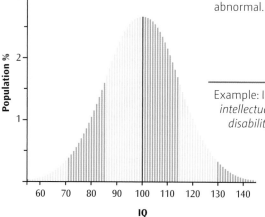

Revision BOOSTER

Questions in the exam which require a description of a definition of abnormality may be worth 2 or 3 marks. Therefore it makes sense to identify three key things you would say for each definition (as we have done here). In an exam, if you write these three things and explain each one, you would certainly get the full 3 marks (except if the question was worth 2 marks – then leave one thing out).

Deviation from social norms

Abnormality is based on social context.	When a person behaves in a way that is different from how they are expected to behave they may be defined as abnormal.
	Societies and social groups make collective judgements about 'correct' behaviours in particular circumstances.
Three types of consequences of behaviour.	There are relatively few behaviours that would be considered universally abnormal therefore definitions are related to cultural context.
	This includes historical differences within the same society.
	For example, homosexuality is viewed as abnormal in some cultures but not others and was considered abnormal in our society in the past.
Example: *antisocial personality disorder.*	One important symptom of antisocial personality disorder (formerly psychopathy) is a failure to conform to 'lawful and culturally normative ethical behaviour'.
	In other words, a psychopath is abnormal because they deviate from social norms or standards. They generally lack empathy.

Abnormality can be defined as behaviour that is statistically infrequent or behaviour that doesn't fit with social norms.

One strength of statistical infrequency is its real-world application.

Statistical infrequency is useful in diagnosis, e.g. intellectual disability disorder because this requires an IQ in the bottom 2%.	It is also helpful in assessing a range of conditions, e.g. the BDI assesses depression, only 5% of people score 30+ (= severe depression).	This means that statistical infrequency is useful in diagnostic and assessment processes.

One limitation is that unusual characteristics can also be positive.

If very few people display a characteristic, then the behaviour is statistically infrequent but doesn't mean we would call them abnormal.	IQ scores above 130 are just as unusual as those below 70, but not regarded as undesirable or needing treatment.	This means that, although statistical infrequency can be part of defining abnormality, it can never be its sole basis.

Evaluation extra: Benefits versus problems.

When someone is living a happy and fulfilled life, there is no benefit to them being labelled as abnormal.	However the label of abnormality, e.g. intellectual disability disorder, might carry a social stigma.	This means that labelling someone abnormal just because they are statistically unusual is likely to do more harm than good.

One strength of deviation from social norms is its real-world application.

Deviation from social norms is useful in the diagnosis of antisocial personality disorder because this requires failure to conform to ethical standards.	Deviation from social norms is also helpful in diagnosing schizotypal personality disorder which involves 'strange' beliefs and behaviour.	This means that deviation from social norms is useful in psychiatric diagnosis.

One limitation is that social norms are situationally and culturally relative.

A person from one culture may label someone from another culture as abnormal using their standards rather than the person's standards.	For example, hearing voices is socially acceptable in some cultures but would be seen as a sign of abnormality in the UK.	This means it is difficult to judge deviation from social norms from one context to another.

Evaluation extra: Human rights abuses.

Reliance on deviation from social norms to understand abnormality can lead to abuse of human rights e.g. nymphomania (as a disorder) to control female behaviour.	However, we need to be able to use deviation from social norms to diagnose conditions such as antisocial personality disorder.	This suggests that, overall, the use of deviation from social norms to define abnormality may do more harm than good because of the potential for abuse.

Apply it

Gloria is a 12-year-old girl who has a very high IQ (in the top 1% of the population). But many people have commented on her poor social skills. She gets uncomfortably close to people in conversation, and makes hurtful and offensive comments (e.g. about someone's appearance). She maintains eye contact for long periods, and appears to have no fear of strangers.

1. Using the statistical infrequency and deviation from social norms definitions, explain why Gloria could be considered abnormal.
2. Are there any reasons why Gloria should not be regarded as abnormal? Explain **at least two** of them.

Revision BOOSTER

On the left there are three evaluation points for each definition of abnormality. It is unlikely that you would be asked to write about just one definition in an extended writing question – but, if you were, then three well-developed points would be enough even for a 16-mark question.

However, if you wanted a fourth you could make a comparison with another definition of abnormality.

Knowledge Check

1. Outline **two** definitions of abnormality. *(6 marks)*
2. Explain **one** strength of statistical infrequency as a definition of abnormality. *(3 marks)*
3. Briefly evaluate the deviation from social norms definition of abnormality. *(4 marks)*
4. Outline **and** evaluate statistical infrequency **and** deviation from social norms as definitions of abnormality. *(12 marks AS, 16 marks AL)*

Definitions of abnormality (2)

Spec spotlight

Definitions of abnormality, including failure to function adequately and deviation from ideal mental health.

At a festival, most people will fail to maintain basic standards of nutrition and hygiene.

Apply it

Stephen Gough is a former Royal Marine known as 'the Naked Rambler' because he spends most of his time walking across Britain wearing nothing more than socks, boots, a rucksack and a hat. He has been arrested more than 20 times and spent almost eight of the last nine years in prison. He has refused to wear clothes at many of his trials. Mr Gough is rational and lucid about his reasons for behaving like this. He does not go out of his way to offend people. He believes it is his human right to go where he likes without clothes.

1. In terms of failure to function adequately and deviation from ideal mental health, would you say that Stephen Gough should be considered abnormal?

2. Explain your answer with reference to psychological concepts.

Revision BOOSTER

Some students find it difficult to remember which definition is which – try to focus less on the word 'deviation' or 'failure' and more on 'statistical', 'social norms', 'function adequately' and 'mental health'.

Failure to function adequately

Inability to cope with everyday living.	A person may cross the line between normal and abnormal at the point that they cannot deal with the demands of everyday life – they fail to function adequately. For instance, not being able to maintain basic standards of nutrition and hygiene, hold down a job or maintain relationships.
Rosenhan and Seligman (1989) proposed further signs of failure to cope.	When someone is not coping: • They no longer conform to interpersonal rules, e.g. maintaining personal space. • They experience severe personal distress. • They behave in a way that is irrational or dangerous.
Example: *intellectual disability disorder.*	Having a very low IQ is a statistical infrequency (see previous spread) but diagnosis would not be made on this basis alone. There would have to be clear signs that the person was not able to cope with the demands of everyday living. So intellectual disability disorder is an example of failure to function adequately.

Deviation from ideal mental health

Look at what is normal.	A different way to look at normality and abnormality is to think about what makes someone 'normal' and psychologically healthy. Then identify anyone who deviates from this ideal.
Jahoda listed 8 criteria.	Jahoda (1958) suggested the following criteria for ideal mental health: 1. We have no symptoms or distress. 2. We are rational and perceive ourselves accurately. 3. We self-actualise. 4. We can cope with stress. 5. We have a realistic view of the world. 6. We have good self-esteem and lack guilt. 7. We are independent of other people. 8. We can successfully work, love and enjoy our leisure.
Inevitable overlap between definitions.	Someone's inability to keep a job may be a sign of their failure to cope with the pressures of work (failure to function). Or as a deviation from the ideal of successfully working.

One strength of failure to function is as a threshold for professional help.

In any given year 25% of us experience symptoms of mental disorder to some degree (Mind).

Most of the time we press on, but when we cease to function adequately people seek or are referred for professional help.

This means that the failure to function criterion provides a way to target treatment and services to those who need them most.

One limitation is this definition can lead to discrimination / social control.

It is hard to distinguish between failure to function and a conscious decision to deviate from social norms.

For example people may choose to live off-grid as part of an alternative lifestyle choice or take part in high-risk leisure activities.

This means that people who make unusual choices can be labelled abnormal and their freedom of choice restricted.

Evaluation extra: Failure to function can be normal.

In some circumstances most of us can't cope e.g. bereavement. It is unfair to give someone a label for reacting normally to difficult circumstances.

On the other hand failure to function is real regardless of the circumstances. A person may need professional help to adjust to bereavement.

This means it is hard to know when to base a judgement of abnormality on failure to function.

One strength of the ideal mental health approach is being comprehensive.

Ideal mental health includes a range of criteria for mental health. It covers most of the reasons why we might need help with mental health.

This means that mental health can be discussed meaningfully with a range of professionals e.g. psychiatrist or CBT therapist.

Therefore ideal mental health provides a checklist against which we can assess ourselves and others.

One limitation is the definition may be culture-bound.

Some criteria for ideal mental health are limited to the US and Europe, e.g. self-actualisation is not recognised in most of the world.

Even in Europe there are variations in the value placed on independence (high in Germany, low in Italy).

This means that it is very difficult to apply the concept of ideal mental health from one culture to another.

Evaluation extra: Extremely high standards.

Few of us attain all Jahoda's criteria for mental health, and none of us maintain them for long. An impossible set of standards can be disheartening.

On the other hand having such comprehensive criteria for mental health might be of value to someone wanting to improve their mental health.

This means that a set of comprehensive criteria for ideal mental health may be helpful for some but not others.

Revision BOOSTER

Do not feel you have to memorise the evaluation points here – the explanations are meant to show the kind of detail you need to go into to fully elaborate your points. Trying to memorise all the details may just mean you end up with too much in your head. Just try to understand the *process* of elaboration.

Good luck with that, son. Some people have suggested that Jahoda's criteria might be a little unrealistic.

Knowledge Check

1. Identify **three** criteria for ideal mental health. *(3 marks)*
2. Outline **and** briefly evaluate the failure to function adequately definition of abnormality. *(6 marks)*
3. Briefly discuss **one** limitation of deviation from ideal mental health. *(4 marks)*
4. Discuss the failure to function adequately **and/or** deviation from ideal mental health definitions of abnormality. *(12 marks AS level, 16 marks AL)*
5. Discuss **two or more** definitions of abnormality. *(12 marks AS, 16 marks AL)*

Phobias, depression and OCD

Spec spotlight

The behavioural, emotional and cognitive characteristics of phobias, depression and obsessive-compulsive disorder (OCD).

Genuphobia is fear of knees. Apologies to those with this phobia.

Apply it

Ramon has been experiencing a lot of stress at work recently. He is lethargic and has no energy or enthusiasm for anything anymore. He can't concentrate on even the simplest tasks. He stares into space a lot just mulling over very negative thoughts, some of which make him anxious. He feels very down, finds it hard to get up in the morning and is eating more and putting on weight. Several times in the past month he has either been late for work or taken the day off.

1. Identify the behavioural, cognitive **and** emotional aspects of Ramon's state.
2. Do you think he is experiencing depression? Explain your answer.
3. Explain why Ramon is unlikely to be experiencing a phobia or OCD.

Phobias

BEHAVIOURAL	Panic. May involve a range of behaviours such as crying, screaming or running away from the phobic stimulus.
	Avoidance. Considerable effort to prevent contact with the phobic stimulus. This can make it hard to go about everyday life.
	Endurance. An alternative behaviour to avoidance. Involves remaining with the phobic stimulus and continuing to experience anxiety.
EMOTIONAL	Anxiety. An unpleasant state of high arousal. Prevents an individual relaxing and makes it very difficult to experience positive emotion.
	Fear. The immediate response we experience when we encounter or think about a phobic stimulus.
	Emotional response is unreasonable. Disproportionate to the threat posed, e.g. a person with arachnophobia will have a strong emotional response to a tiny spider.
COGNITIVE	Selective attention to the phobic stimulus. A person with a phobia finds it hard to look away from the phobic stimulus.
	Irrational beliefs. Phobias may involve beliefs e.g. 'if I blush people will think I'm weak'.
	Cognitive distortions. Unrealistic thinking, e.g. belly buttons appear ugly.

Depression

BEHAVIOURAL	Activity levels. People with depression have reduced levels of energy making them lethargic e.g. cannot get out of bed.
	Disruption to sleep and eating behaviour. Reduced sleep (insomnia) or increased (hypersomnia). Appetite and weight may increase or decrease.
	Aggression and self-harm. Depression is associated with irritability and this may extend to aggression and self-harm.
EMOTIONAL	Lowered mood. People with depression describe themselves as 'worthless' or 'empty'.
	Anger. Such emotions lead to aggression or self-harming behaviour.
	Lowered self-esteem. The person likes themselves less, even self-loathing.

Obsessive-compulsive disorder (OCD)

BEHAVIOURAL	**Compulsions are repetitive.** Actions carried out repeatedly in a ritualistic way, e.g. hand-washing.
	Compulsions reduce anxiety. Anxiety may be created by obsessions, or just anxiety alone.
	Avoidance. OCD is managed by avoiding situations that trigger anxiety, e.g. avoid rubbish bins because they have germs.
EMOTIONAL	**Anxiety and distress.** Obsessive thoughts are unpleasant and frightening, and the anxiety that goes with these can be overwhelming.
	Depression. Low mood and lack of enjoyment.
	Guilt and disgust. Irrational guilt, for example over a minor moral issue, or disgust which is directed towards oneself or something external like dirt.
COGNITIVE	**Obsessive thoughts.** About 90% of people with OCD have recurring intrusive thoughts e.g. about being contaminated by dirt or germs.
	Cognitive coping strategies. Some people with OCD use strategies to cope e.g. meditation.
	Insight into excessive anxiety. Awareness that thoughts and behaviour are irrational. May have catastrophic thoughts and be hypervigilant.

COGNITIVE	**Poor concentration.** The person may find themselves unable to stick with a task, or might find simple decision-making difficult.
	Attention to the negative. Depressed people have a bias towards focusing on negative aspects of current situations and recalling unhappy (instead of happy) memories.
	Absolutist thinking. 'Black-and-white thinking', when a situation is unfortunate it is seen as an absolute disaster.

Revision BOOSTER

This spread deals with the characteristics of phobias, depression and OCD. Questions on this section are likely to be either descriptive or application. There isn't really scope for evaluative material here.

For each characteristic/symptom you describe, first identify it clearly before going on to describe it in detail. Use examples as a means of providing more detail.

Hypervigilance – keeping attention focused on potential hazards. Unfortunately, Norris wasn't the most hypervigilant.

Knowledge Check

1. Outline how a person's emotional state may change in response to OCD. *(4 marks)*
2. Identify **one** emotional, **one** behavioural **and one** cognitive characteristic of OCD. *(3 marks)*
3. Using the example of someone with a phobia of birds, explain the characteristics of a phobia. *(6 marks)*
4. Explain cognitive **or** emotional characteristics of depression. *(4 marks)*
5. Outline the likely behavioural characteristics of someone who has been diagnosed with depression. *(6 marks)*

Spec spotlight

The behavioural approach to explaining phobias: the two-process model, including classical and operant conditioning.

The behavioural approach is the same as behaviourism, which is described on page 72.

Phobia

Unconditioned stimulus (UCS) →	Unconditioned response (UCR)
Being bitten	**Anxiety**

Neutral stimulus (NS) →	No response
Dog	

UCS + NS →	UCR
Being bitten + dog	**Anxiety**

Conditioned stimulus (CS) →	Conditioned response (CR)
Dog	**Anxiety**

Revision BOOSTER

If studies are used as evaluation, you should include very little description of procedures. But studies can also be used for descriptive content and then the procedures are relevant – here they act as an example of how classical conditioning works.

The Little Albert study. Some experts have questioned the authenticity of this photograph.

The two-process model

Classical conditioning and operant conditioning.	Mowrer (1960) argued that phobias are learned by classical conditioning and then maintained by operant conditioning, i.e. two processes are involved.
Acquisition by classical conditioning.	Classical conditioning involves association. 1. **UCS** triggers a fear response (fear is a **UCR**), e.g. being bitten creates anxiety. 2. **NS** is associated with the UCS, e.g. being bitten by a dog (the dog previously did not create anxiety). 3. NS becomes a **CS** producing fear (which is now the **CR**). The dog becomes a CS causing a CR of anxiety/fear following the bite.
Little Albert: conditioned fear.	Watson and Rayner (1920) showed how a fear of rats could be conditioned in 'Little Albert'. 1. Whenever Albert played with a white rat, a loud noise was made close to his ear. The noise (UCS) caused a fear response (UCR). 2. Rat (NS) did not create fear until the bang and the rat had been paired together several times. 3. Albert showed a fear response (CR) every time he came into contact with the rat (now a CS).
Generalisation of fear to other stimuli.	For example, Little Albert also showed a fear in response to other white furry objects including a fur coat and a Santa Claus beard.
Maintenance by operant conditioning (*negative reinforcement*).	Operant conditioning takes place when our behaviour is reinforced or punished. Negative reinforcement – an individual produces behaviour that avoids something unpleasant. When a person with a phobia avoids a phobic stimulus they escape the anxiety that would have been experienced. This reduction in fear negatively reinforces the avoidance behaviour and the phobia is maintained.
Example of negative reinforcement.	If someone has a morbid fear of clowns (coulrophobia) they will avoid circuses and other situations where they may encounter clowns. The relief felt from avoiding clowns negatively reinforces the phobia and ensures it is maintained rather than confronted.

One strength of the two-process model is its real-world application.

The idea that phobias are maintained by avoidance is important in explaining why people with phobias benefit from exposure therapies (e.g. SD on next spread).

Once avoidance behaviour is prevented it ceases to be reinforced by the reduction of anxiety. Avoidance behaviour therefore declines.

This shows the value of the two-process approach because it identifies a means of treating phobias.

One limitation is the inability to explain cognitive aspects of phobias.

Behavioural explanations like the two-process model are geared towards explaining *behaviour* – in this case avoidance of the phobic stimulus.

However, we know that phobias also have a significant **cognitive** component, e.g. people hold irrational beliefs about the phobic stimulus.

This means that the two-process model does not fully explain the symptoms of phobias.

Another strength is evidence linking phobias to bad experiences.

De Jongh *et al.* (2006) found that 73% of dental phobics had experienced a trauma (mostly involving dentistry), evidence of link between bad experiences and phobias.

Further support came from the control group of people with low dental anxiety, where only 21% had experienced a traumatic event.

This confirms that the association between stimulus (dentistry) and an **unconditioned response** (pain) does lead to the phobia.

Counterpoint

Not all phobias appear following a bad experience. Snake phobias still occur in populations where very few people have any experience of snakes. Also, not all frightening experiences lead to phobias.

This means that behavioural theories probably do not provide an explanation for all cases of phobia.

Evaluation extra: Learning and evolution.

The two-process model provides a credible explanation for how a person might develop and maintain a particular phobia.

However, preparedness is an alternative explanation. This is the tendency to develop phobias for things that presented a danger in our evolutionary past (e.g snakes and the dark).

This means that the two-process model does not explain some important properties of phobias.

Do you agree with this conclusion?

Apply it

Marina has acrophobia, an irrational fear of heights. She hates even climbing the stairs at home and can't look out of the upstairs windows. Whenever Marina thinks about heights, she feels sick and starts sweating. She becomes very anxious in situations where she is aware of being 'off the ground', so she tries her best to avoid them but this is seriously interfering with her life.

1. Use the two-process model to explain how Marina's acrophobia was acquired **and** how it is maintained. In your explanation, refer to **both** classical **and** operant conditioning.

2. Explain **one** reason why this may not be an adequate explanation of Marina's acrophobia.

Phobias such as claustrophobia and agoraphobia can have serious effects on everyday living.

Knowledge Check

1. One way a phobia can develop is through classical conditioning. Explain how classical conditioning could account for the development of a phobia of clowns. *(4 marks)*

2. Outline the two-process model of phobias. *(4 marks)*

3. Briefly evaluate the two-process model as an explanation for phobias. *(4 marks)*

4. Describe **and** evaluate the two-process model of phobias. *(12 marks AS, 16 marks AL)*

The behavioural approach to treating phobias

Spec spotlight

The behavioural approach to treating phobias: systematic desensitisation, including relaxation and use of hierarchy, flooding.

Apply it

Marina's acrophobia (fear of heights) is causing her such inconvenience and anxiety that she decides to get some help. She is referred to a clinical psychologist who uses systematic desensitisation to treat her phobia.

1. Explain practical ways in which each of the following would be included in Marina's treatment: (a) anxiety hierarchy, (b) relaxation, (c) exposure.

2. Marina isn't sure that systematic desensitisation is the best treatment for her phobia. Explain how she could be treated using an alternative behavioural therapy.

Not that kind of flooding. Unless you have a fear of water – in which case, welcome to the treatment room...

Systematic desensitisation (SD)

Based on **classical conditioning**, *counterconditioning* and *reciprocal inhibition*.	The therapy aims to gradually reduce anxiety through counterconditioning: • Phobia is learned so that phobic stimulus (**conditioned stimulus**, **CS**) produces fear (**conditioned response**, **CR**). • CS is paired with relaxation and this becomes the new CR. *Reciprocal inhibition* – not possible to be afraid and relaxed at the same time, so one emotion prevents the other.
Formation of an *anxiety hierarchy*.	Client and therapist design an anxiety hierarchy – fearful stimuli arranged in order from least to most frightening. A person with arachnophobia might identify seeing a picture of a small spider as low on their anxiety hierarchy and holding a tarantula as the final item.
Relaxation practised at each level of the hierarchy.	Person with phobia is first taught relaxation techniques such as deep breathing and/or meditation. Person then works through the anxiety hierarchy. At each level the person is exposed to the phobic stimulus in a relaxed state. This takes place over several sessions starting at the bottom of the hierarchy. Treatment is successful when the person can stay relaxed in high-anxiety situations.

Flooding

Immediate exposure to the phobic stimulus.	Flooding involves exposing a person with a phobia with the phobic object without a gradual build-up. A person with arachnophobia receiving flooding treatment may have a large spider crawl over their hand until they can relax fully (the person not the spider).
Very quick learning through extinction.	Without the option of avoidance behaviour, the person quickly learns that the phobic object is harmless through the exhaustion of their fear response. This is known as extinction.
Ethical safeguards.	Flooding is not unethical but it is an unpleasant experience so it is important that people being treated give **informed consent**. They must be fully prepared and know what to expect.

One strength of SD is evidence of effectiveness.

Gilroy *et al.* (2003) followed up 42 people who had SD for spider phobia. At follow-up, the SD group were less fearful than a **control group**.

In a recent review Wechsler *et al.* (2019) concluded that SD is effective for specific phobia, social phobia and agoraphobia.

This means that SD is likely to be helpful for people with phobias.

Another strength is SD's usefulness for people with learning disabilities.

Main alternatives to SD are unsuitable for people with learning disabilities, e.g. **cognitive** therapies require a high level of rational thought and flooding is distressing.

SD, on the other hand, does not require understanding or engagement on a cognitive level and is not a traumatic experience.

This means that SD is often the most appropriate treatment for some people.

Evaluation extra: SD in virtual reality.

The exposure part of SD can be done in virtual reality (VR) which avoids dangerous situations (e.g. heights) and is cost-effective.

However VR exposure may be less effective than real exposure for social phobias because it lacks realism (Wechsler *et al.* 2019).

This means that SD using VR is sometimes but not always appropriate.

One strength of flooding is that it is cost-effective.

A therapy is described as cost-effective if it is clinically effective and not expensive. Flooding can work in as little as one session.

Even with a longer session (e.g. three hours) this makes flooding more cost-effective than alternatives.

This means that more people can be treated at the same cost by flooding than by SD or other therapies.

One limitation of flooding is that it is traumatic.

Schumacher *et al.* (2015) found that both participants and therapists rated flooding as more stressful than SD.

Thus there are ethical concerns about knowingly causing stress (offset by informed consent), and the traumatic nature of flooding also leads to higher **attrition** rates than for SD.

This suggests that, overall, therapists may avoid using this treatment.

Evaluation extra: Symptom substitution.

Behavioural therapies do not treat causes so symptoms reappear, e.g. woman with death phobia which turned into fear of criticism (Persons 1986).

However, the only evidence for symptom substitution comes in the form of case studies which may not **generalise** to all cases and phobias.

This means that symptom substitution is largely a theoretical idea and there is only relatively poor empirical evidence to support it.

Revision BOOSTER

There are two named treatments on the specification for the behavioural approach, so if both treatments are the focus of an essay, do not over-describe one at the expense of the other and don't spend too long on the description at the expense of the evaluation.

Comparison between treatments/ therapies is an excellent way to gain AO3 marks – and it's possible you may be asked to do this as part of an essay. Make a list of similarities and differences between systematic desensitisation and flooding and try to explain these in more detail.

It was at that point that Belinda wondered if the final stage of the anxiety hierarchy to cure her fear of the dentist had perhaps come a little too soon...

Knowledge Check

1. Outline **one** behavioural approach to treating phobias.
   (4 marks)

2. Discuss **two** reasons why systematic desensitisation might be a more successful treatment for phobias than flooding. *(6 marks)*

3. Briefly evaluate flooding as a treatment for phobias. *(4 marks)*

4. Describe **and** evaluate **one or more** behavioural approaches to treating phobias.
   (12 marks AS, 16 marks AL)

The cognitive approach to explaining depression

Spec spotlight

The cognitive approach to explaining depression: Beck's negative triad and Ellis's ABC model.

Depression. Not a laughing matter – literally or metaphorically.

Revision BOOSTER

The essay question you are most likely to be asked would be about the cognitive approach to explaining depression in general, rather than either Beck or Ellis alone. In such a case you should be careful not to spend too much time on description because the evaluation is at least as important as the description. However, it is possible that one essay might be on Beck or Ellis individually, so prepare that as well.

Apply it

Rosie recently failed a mock A level exam. She feels very down about it and is experiencing other symptoms of depression too. She thinks she is useless and worthless, and feels guilty for letting everyone down. She now finds she can't motivate herself to work or do anything to improve next time.

1. Explain Rosie's depression in terms of Beck's negative triad.

2. In Ellis's terms, identify **and** explain the ABC of Rosie's experience.

Beck (1967) Negative triad

Faulty information processing.	Beck (1967) suggested that some people are more prone to depression because of faulty information processing, i.e. thinking in a flawed way.
	When depressed people attend to the negative aspects of a situation and ignore positives, they also tend to blow small problems out of proportion and think in 'black-and-white' terms.
Depressed people have negative *self-schema*.	A *schema* is a 'package' of ideas and information developed through experience. We use schema to interpret the world, so if a person has a negative self-schema they interpret *all* information about themselves in a negative way.
The *negative triad*.	There are three elements to the negative triad: • *Negative view of the world*, e.g. 'the world is a cold hard place'. • *Negative view of the future*, e.g. 'there isn't much chance that the economy will get any better'. • *Negative view of the self*, e.g. thinking 'I am a failure' and this negatively impacts upon self-esteem.

Ellis (1962) ABC model

A Activating event	Ellis suggested that depression arises from *irrational thoughts*. According to Ellis depression occurs when we experience negative events, e.g. failing an important test or ending a relationship.
B Beliefs	Negative events trigger irrational beliefs, for example: • Ellis called the belief that we *must* always succeed *musterbation*. • *I-can't-stand-it-itis* is the belief that it is a disaster when things do not go smoothly. • *Utopianism* is the belief that the world must always be fair and just.
C Consequences	When an activating event triggers irrational beliefs there are emotional and behavioural consequences. For example, if you believe you must always succeed and then you fail at something, the consequence is depression.

One strength of Beck's model is supporting research.

Clark and Beck (1999) concluded that cognitive vulnerabilities (e.g. faulty information processing, negative self-schema) are more common in depressed people.

A recent prospective study by Cohen *et al.* (2019) tracked 473 adolescents' development and found that early cognitive vulnerability predicted later depression.

This shows that there is an association between cognitive vulnerability and depression.

Another strength is real-world application to screening for depression.

Assessing cognitive vulnerability in young people most at risk of developing depression means they can be monitored.

Understanding cognitive vulnerability is applied in CBT to alter cognitions underlying depression, making a person more resilient to life events.

This means that the idea of cognitive vulnerability is useful in clinical practice.

Evaluation extra: A partial explanation.

Depressed people show particular patterns of cognition, even before the onset of depression. Therefore Beck's idea of cognitive vulnerability is at least a partial explanation.

However, some aspects of depression are not explained by cognitive factors. These include experiences of extreme anger, and for some people hallucinations and delusions.

This suggests that the cognitive model is not a particularly good explanation for all depressive phenomena.

'I must succeed at everything'...
'Everyone must like me.' Ellis called this 'musterbating'. Be a bit careful how you write that in the exam.

One strength of Ellis's model is its application in treating depression.

Ellis applied the ABC model to treat depression (rational emotive behaviour therapy, REBT).

Evidence that REBT can both change negative beliefs and relieve the symptoms of depression (David *et al.* 2018).

This means that REBT has real-world value.

One limitation is Ellis's model only explains reactive depression.

Reactive depression describes a form of depression which is triggered by negative activating events.

However, in many cases it is not obvious what triggers depression, described as endogenous depression. Ellis's model is less useful in explaining this.

This means that Ellis's model can only explain some cases of depression.

Evaluation extra: Ethical issues.

The ABC model of depression locates responsibility for depression with the depressed person. Critics see this as blaming the depressed person.

However, the application of the ABC model to REBT (see next spread) does appear to make at least some depressed people achieve more resilience and feel better.

This means that REBT gives reason for concern but can be ethically acceptable as long as it is carried out sensitively to avoid victim-blaming.

Knowledge Check

1. Identify the **three** key elements of Beck's negative triad **and** illustrate each with an example. *(6 marks)*

2. Outline Ellis's ABC model as an explanation for depression. *(4 marks)*

3. Briefly evaluate the cognitive approach to explaining depression. *(6 marks)*

4. Maria recently failed her driving test. She says the test was unfair and the examiner was 'out to get her'. She says she hates herself and will never try anything again. Before the test Maria told her friend that she had to pass otherwise she could not go on. Maria's friend thinks she might be showing signs of depression.

   Describe **and** evaluate the cognitive approach to explaining depression. Refer to Maria in your answer. *(12 marks AS, 16 marks AL)*

The cognitive approach to treating depression

Spec spotlight

The cognitive approach to treating depression: cognitive behaviour therapy (CBT), including challenging irrational thoughts.

Revision BOOSTER

If you are asked to discuss the cognitive approach to treating depression, be careful not to include material on cognitive *explanations*. This is easily done – especially as the treatments are based on the assumptions of the explanations, but such material wouldn't get any credit.

Apply it

Rosie (from the previous spread) is being treated for depression by a cognitive behaviour therapist, who believes the key to successful treatment is to challenge Rosie's irrational thoughts.

1. **Explain how the therapist might do this.**

Rosie isn't sure how useful CBT is, so she comes to you for advice.

2. **What would you tell her?**

Ellis used to encourage his clients to take part in 'shame attacking exercises' such as taking a banana for a walk on a lead in a busy shopping centre. As his clients did so Ellis would remind them to think, 'What's the worst that could happen?'

Cognitive behaviour therapy (CBT)

Most common psychological treatment e.g. for depression.	CBT is an example of the **cognitive** approach to treatment, though it also includes behavioural aspects. • Cognitive – challenge negative, irrational thoughts. • Behaviour – change behaviour so it is more effective. Client and therapist work together.
Beck – challenge *negative thoughts*.	The aim is to identify negative thoughts about the self, the world and the future – the negative triad. These thoughts must be challenged by the client taking an active role in their treatment.
The 'client as scientist'.	Clients are encouraged to test the reality of their irrational beliefs. They might be set homework, e.g. to record when they enjoyed an event. This is referred to as the 'client as scientist'. In future sessions if clients say that no one is nice to them, the therapist can produce this evidence to prove the client's beliefs are incorrect.
Ellis's rational emotive behaviour therapy (REBT).	REBT extends the ABC model to an *ABCDE model*: • D for dispute (challenge) irrational beliefs. • E for effect.
Challenging *irrational thoughts*.	A client might talk about how unlucky they have been or how unfair life is. An REBT therapist would identify this as *utopianism* and challenge it as irrational. • *Empirical argument* – disputing whether there is evidence to support the irrational belief. • *Logical argument* – disputing whether the negative thought actually follows from the facts.
Behavioural activation.	As individuals become depressed, they tend to increasingly avoid difficult situations and become isolated, which maintains or worsens symptoms. The goal of behavioural activation, therefore, is to work with depressed individuals to gradually decrease their avoidance and isolation, and increase their engagement in activities that have been shown to improve mood, e.g. exercising, going out to dinner, etc.

One strength of CBT is that there is evidence of effectiveness.

March et al. (2007) compared the effects of CBT with *antidepressant* drugs and a combination of the two in 327 depressed adolescents.

After 36 weeks 81% of CBT group, 81% of antidepressants group and 86% of CBT + antidepressants group were significantly improved.

This means there is a good case for making CBT the first choice of treatment in public health care systems like the NHS.

Revision BOOSTER

Note that some of these evaluation points apply to cognitive therapies in general rather than being specifically applied to Beck or Ellis. This is good as a shorter 'describe and evaluate' question – say *8 marks* – on Ellis or Beck would mean that you could use some of the same points in either case.

One limitation is suitability for diverse clients.

In severe cases depressed clients may not be able to motivate themselves to engage with the cognitive work of CBT. They may not even be able to pay attention in a session.

Sturmey (2005) suggests that any form of psychotherapy (including CBT) is not suitable for people with learning difficulties.

This means that CBT may only be appropriate for a specific range of clients.

Counterpoint

There is now evidence to challenge this conventional wisdom. Lewis and Lewis (2016) concluded that CBT was as effective as other treatments for severe depression. Taylor et al. (2008) concluded that CBT can be effective for people with learning disabilities.

This means that CBT may have much wider application than was once thought.

It may be the quality of the therapist–client relationship that determines the success of therapy. Bad news for these two...

One limitation of CBT is its high relapse rates.

Few early studies looked at long-term effectiveness and recent studies suggest that relapse is common.

Ali et al. (2017) assessed depression for 12 months following a course of CBT. 42% relapsed within six months of ending treatment and 53% within a year.

This means that CBT may need to be repeated periodically.

Not everyone agrees with this conclusion. What do you think?

Evaluation extra: Client preference.

There is a large body of evidence to show that, used appropriately, CBT is highly effective, at least in the short term, in tackling symptoms of depression.

However, some clients prefer to take medication or explore the past, some rate CBT as least preferred therapy (Yrondi et al. 2015).

This suggests that people, even those who are depressed, should have the right to choose their therapy even if it may not be the one with the best evidence of effectiveness.

Knowledge Check

1. Explain **one** strength of using cognitive behaviour therapy to treat depression. *(3 marks)*

2. Explain how irrational thoughts are challenged as part of the cognitive approach to treating depression. *(2 marks)*

3. Outline **and** evaluate **one** cognitive approach to treating depression. *(8 marks)*

4. Describe **and** evaluate the cognitive approach to explaining **and** treating depression. *(12 marks AS, 16 marks AL)*

The biological approach to explaining OCD

Spec spotlight

The biological approach to explaining OCD: genetic and neural explanations.

Could an obsession with cleanliness be 'all in the genes'? Perhaps, judging by these two.

Apply it

Dilip is a middle-aged man who has OCD, especially intrusive thoughts about contamination. He wants to find out what causes it, and recalls that his dad used to compulsively wash himself and clean the house. Dilip is concerned that his children might also have OCD.

1. How would you explain the genetic causes of OCD to Dilip?

2. What could you tell Dilip about the role of the brain in OCD?

Revision BOOSTER

There are two biological approaches to explaining OCD identified in the specification (genetic and neural). This means you could be set a question on biological approaches to explaining OCD in general or on each explanation specifically. We have only provided three AO1 points for each so you will need to ensure you make the most of these should separate essays be set.

Genetic explanations

Candidate *genes* e.g. 5HT1-D.	Researchers have identified specific genes which create a vulnerability for OCD, called candidate genes. • **Serotonin** genes, e.g. 5HT1-D beta, are implicated in the transmission of serotonin across *synapses*. • **Dopamine** genes are also implicated in OCD and may regulate mood. Both dopamine and serotonin are *neurotransmitters*.
OCD is *polygenic*.	OCD is not caused by one single gene but several genes are involved. Taylor (2013) found evidence that up to 230 different genes may be involved in OCD.
Different types of OCD.	One group of genes may cause OCD in one person but a different group of genes may cause the disorder in another person – known as *aetiologically heterogeneous*. There is also evidence that different types of OCD may be the result of particular genetic variations, such as hoarding disorder and religious obsession.

Neural explanations

Low levels of *serotonin* lowers mood.	Neurotransmitters are responsible for relaying information from one *neuron* to another. For example if a person has low levels of serotonin then normal transmission of mood-relevant information does not take place and mood (and sometimes other mental processes) is affected.
Decision-making systems in *frontal lobes* impaired.	Some cases of OCD, and in particular hoarding disorder, seem to be associated with impaired decision-making. This is turn may be associated with abnormal functioning of the lateral (side bits) frontal lobes of the brain. The frontal lobes are responsible for logical thinking and making decisions.
Parahippocampal gyrus dysfunctional.	There is also evidence to suggest that an area called the left parahippocampal gyrus, associated with processing unpleasant emotions, functions abnormally in OCD.

One strength is evidence for the genetic explanation of OCD.

Nestadt *et al.* (2010) reviewed twin studies and found that 68% of identical twins (MZ) shared OCD as opposed to 31% of non-identical (DZ) twins.

Marini and Stebnicki (2012) found that a person with a family member with OCD is around four times as likely to develop it as someone without.

This means that people who are genetically similar are more likely to share OCD, supporting a role for genetic vulnerability.

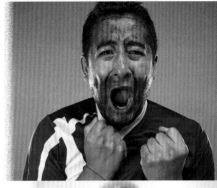

One limitation is the existence of environmental risk factors.

Genetic variation affects vulnerability to OCD, but there are also environmental risk factors that trigger or increase the risk of OCD.

Cromer *et al.* (2007) found in one sample over half of people with OCD experienced a traumatic event. OCD severity correlated positively with number of traumas.

This means that genetic vulnerability only provides a partial explanation for OCD.

Evaluation extra: Animal studies.

Evidence from animal studies show particular genes are associated with repetitive behaviours in other species (e.g. mice, Ahmari 2016).

However, the human mind is much more complex, so it may not be possible to **generalise** from animal repetitive behaviour to human OCD.

This means that animal studies of candidate genes are probably not relevant to understanding OCD.

One strength of the neural model is supporting evidence.

Antidepressants that work on serotonin reduce OCD symptoms. This suggests that serotonin may be involved in OCD.

Also, OCD symptoms form part of conditions that are known to be biological in origin e.g. Parkinson's disease (Nestadt *et al.* 2010).

This means that biological factors (e.g. serotonin and processes underlying Parkinson's disease) are likely to be involved in OCD.

Obsessions or compulsions?

One limitation of the neural model is there is no unique neural system.

Many people with OCD also experience depression. This depression probably involves disruption to the action of serotonin.

It could simply be that serotonin activity is disrupted in many people with OCD because they are depressed as well.

This means that serotonin may not be relevant to OCD symptoms.

Evaluation extra: Correlation and causality.

Some neural systems don't work normally in people with OCD. The biological model suggests this is explained by brain dysfunction *causing* the OCD.

However, this is just a correlation which does not necessarily indicate a causal relationship. OCD (or depression) might cause the abnormal brain function.

This means that there is a lack of strong evidence for a neural basis to OCD though correlations may eventually lead us to a cause.

Download suggested answers to the Knowledge Check questions from tinyurl.com/y8kjyvwe

Knowledge Check

1. Explain the genetic **or** neural explanation for OCD. *(6 marks)*
2. Explain **one** strength of the neural explanation for OCD. *(3 marks)*
3. Briefly outline the biological approach to explaining OCD. *(4 marks)*
4. Describe **and** evaluate research into genetic and neural explanations of OCD. *(12 marks AS, 16 marks AL)*

The biological approach to treating OCD

Spec spotlight

The biological approach to treating OCD: drug therapy.

Ironic that OCD is classed as a 'disorder'. It's all about order.

Revision BOOSTER

For a *detailed* description of drug therapy you should include reference to named examples (as we have here) as well as their specific 'mode of action' (i.e. what they do) in the brain.

Apply it

Dilip eventually visits his GP for help with his OCD. The GP recommends a psychological therapy but Dilip is adamant that he does not want that kind of treatment and wonders if there is a drug he can take instead.

1. Identify which drug Dilip's GP is likely to prescribe **and** suggest how the doctor might explain how the drug will work to treat OCD.

2. Outline **one** argument Dilip's GP might use to persuade him to reconsider his opposition to psychological treatment.

'When you're obsessive, like me, searching for something unattainable can become unhealthy... it's like falling through the air and grabbing at the clouds.'

– Jonny Wilkinson, rugby player

Drug therapy

Changing levels of *neurotransmitters*.	Drug therapy for mental disorders aims to increase or decrease levels of neurotransmitters in the brain or to increase/decrease their activity. Low levels of **serotonin** are associated with OCD. Therefore drugs work in various ways to increase the level of serotonin in the brain.
Selective serotonin reuptake inhibitors (SSRIs).	SSRIs prevent the reabsorption and breakdown of serotonin in the brain. This increases its levels in the synapse and thus serotonin continues to stimulate the *postsynaptic neuron*. This compensates for whatever is wrong with the serotonin system in OCD.
Typical dosage.	A typical daily dose of *fluoxetine* (an SSRI) is 20 mg although this may be increased if it is not benefitting the person. It takes 3–4 months of daily use for SSRIs to impact upon symptoms. Dose can be increased (e.g. 60 mg a day) if this is appropriate.
Combining SSRIs with CBT.	Drugs are often used alongside *cognitive behaviour therapy* (CBT) to treat OCD. The drugs reduce a person's emotional symptoms, such as feeling anxious or depressed. This means that they can engage more effectively with CBT.
Alternatives to SSRIs: *Tricyclics*.	Tricyclics (an older type of antidepressant) are sometimes used, such as *clomipramine*. These have the same effect on the serotonin system as SSRIs but the side-effects can be more severe.
SNRIs.	In the last five years a different class of antidepressant drugs called *serotonin noradrenaline reuptake inhibitors* (SNRIs) has also been used to treat OCD. Like tricyclics these are a second line of defence for people who don't respond to SSRIs. SNRIs increase levels of serotonin as well as *noradrenaline*.

One strength of drug therapy is its effectiveness.

Soomro *et al.* (2009) reviewed 17 studies of SSRIs for the treatment of OCD. All 17 studies showed better outcomes following SSRIs than placebos.

Typically OCD symptoms reduce for around 70% of people taking SSRIs.

This means that drugs can be of help to most people with OCD.

'I do not have OCD, OCD, OCD' –

– Emilie Autumn

Counterpoint

Although drug treatments may be better than placebos, they may not be the most effective treatments. Cognitive and behavioural (exposure) therapies may be more effective than SSRIs in the treatment of OCD (Skapinakis *et al.* 2016).

This means that drugs may not be the optimum treatment for OCD.

Another strength is that drugs are cost-effective and non-disruptive.

A strength of drug treatments for psychological disorders in general is that they are cheap compared to psychological treatments. Using drugs to treat OCD is therefore good value for the NHS.

As compared to psychological therapies, SSRIs are also non-disruptive to people's lives. If you wish you can simply take drugs until your symptoms decline rather than spending time going to therapy sessions.

This means that many doctors and people with OCD prefer drug treatments.

Apparently chocolate can increase levels of serotonin in the brain – 'I'll take one large dose three times a day please doctor...'

One limitation is that drugs can have serious side-effects.

A minority of people taking SSRIs get no benefit. Some people also experience side-effects such as indigestion, blurred vision and loss of sex drive (although these side-effects are usually temporary).

For those taking *clomipramine*, side-effects are more common and can be more serious. More than 1 in 10 people experience erection problems and weight gain, 1 in 100 become aggressive.

This means that people's quality of life is poor and the outcome is they may stop taking the drugs altogether, reducing the effectiveness of the treatment.

Evaluation extra: Biased evidence.

Some psychologists believe that the evidence for effectiveness is biased because of drug company sponsorship (Goldacre 2013).

On the other hand, the best evidence *available* is supportive of the usefulness of drugs for OCD, and evidence for psychological therapies is biased too.

This means that *as far as we know* drugs are helpful for treating OCD, so it may be preferable to continue using them.

Knowledge Check

1. Outline the use of **one or more** drugs in the treatment of OCD. *(4 marks)*
2. Explain **two** strengths of using drug therapy to treat OCD. *(6 marks)*
3. Outline **and** briefly evaluate drug therapy as a treatment for OCD. *(6 marks)*
4. Discuss the biological approach to treating OCD. *(12 marks AS, 16 marks AL)*

Experimental method

Spec spotlight

Experimental method.

Aims: stating aims, the difference between aims and hypotheses.

Hypotheses: directional and non-directional.

Variables: including independent, dependent, extraneous, confounding; operationalisation of variables.

Demand characteristics and investigator effects.

Pilot studies and the aims of piloting.

Control: random allocation and counterbalancing, randomisation and standardisation.

Experimental designs: repeated measures, independent groups, matched pairs.

The term 'research technique' refers to a set of procedures used to collect data as part of psychological research. In some investigations, more than one technique may be used – such as the use of questionnaires to measure the DV in an experiment.

Apply it

In an experiment into forgetting, two groups of participants learned a list of ten words. Each group was then given a new list to learn – either synonyms (words with the same meanings as those in the original list) or nonsense syllables (e.g. CEZ). Both groups then recalled the words from the original list.

1. Write a suitable hypothesis for this study. *(2 marks)*
2. State the operationalised IV and DV for this study. *(2 marks)*
3. Explain how demand characteristics might have influenced this study. *(2 marks)*
4. Explain how randomisation could have been used in this study. *(2 marks)*

Key concepts

Aims.	A general expression of what the researcher intends to investigate.
Operationalised hypotheses.	A statement of what the researcher believes to be true. It should be *operationalised*, i.e. clearly defined and measurable. A *directional hypothesis* states whether changes are greater or lesser, positive or negative, etc. (used when theory/research suggests the direction). A *non-directional hypothesis* doesn't state the direction, just that there is a difference, correlation, association (used when there is no theory/previous research or it is contradictory).
Independent and dependent variables.	A researcher causes the *independent variable* (**IV**) to vary and records the effect of the IV on the *dependent variable* (**DV**). There are different *levels* of the IV.

Research issues

Extraneous and confounding variables.	• **Extraneous variables** (EVs) are 'nuisance' variables that 'muddy the water' and may make it more difficult to detect an effect. A researcher may control some of these.
	• **Confounding variables** (CVs) change systematically with the IV so we cannot be sure if any observed change in the DV is due to the CV or the IV.
Demand characteristics.	Refers to any cue from the researcher or research situation that may reveal the aim of the study, and change participants' behaviour.
Investigator effects.	Any effect of the investigator's behaviour on the outcome of the research (the DV) and also on design decisions.
Randomisation.	The use of chance when designing investigations to control for the effects of bias e.g. allocating participants to conditions.
Standardisation.	Using exactly the same formalised procedures for all participants in a research study, otherwise differences become EVs.

Pilot studies and more

Pilot studies.	Small-scale trial run of an investigation to 'road-test' procedures, so that research design can be modified.
Control groups/ conditions.	Control groups (independent groups design) or **control conditions** (repeated measures design) are used to set comparison. They act as a 'baseline' and help establish causation.
Single blind and double blind.	Single blind – a participant doesn't know the aims of the study so that **demand characteristics** are reduced. Double blind – both participant and researcher don't know the aims of the study to reduce demand characteristics and investigator effects.

Independent groups

One group does condition A and a second group does condition B.
Participants should be **randomly allocated** to **experimental groups**.

⊕ No order effects.	Participants are only tested once so can't practise or become bored/tired.	This controls an important CV.
⊕ Will not guess aim.	Participants only tested once so are unlikely to guess the research aims.	Therefore behaviour may be more 'natural' (higher realism).
⊖ Participant variables.	The participants in the two groups are different, acting as EV/CV.	May reduce the **validity** of the study.
⊖ Less economical.	Need twice as many participants as repeated measures for same data.	More time spent recruiting which is expensive.

Repeated measures

Same participants take part in all conditions of an experiment.
The order of conditions should be **counterbalanced** to avoid order effects.

⊕ Participant variables.	The person in both conditions has the same characteristics.	This controls an important CV.
⊕ Fewer participants.	Half the number of participants is needed than in independent groups.	Less time spent recruiting participants.
⊖ Order effects are a problem.	Participants may do better or worse when doing a similar task twice. Also practice/ fatigue effects.	Reduces the validity of the results.
⊖ Participants guess aims.	Participants may change their behaviour.	This may reduce the validity of the results.

Matched pairs

Two groups of participants are used but they are also related to each other by being paired on *participant variable*(s) that matter for the experiment.

⊕ Participant variables.	Participants matched on a variable that is relevant to the experiment.	This controls participant variables and enhances the validity of the results.
⊕ No order effects.	Participants are only tested once so no practice or fatigue effects.	This enhances the validity of the results.
⊖ Matching is not perfect.	Matching is time-consuming and can't control all relevant variables.	Cannot address all participant variables.
⊖ More participants.	Need twice as many participants as repeated measures for same data.	More time spent recruiting which is expensive.

Participant variables refer to characteristics of the participants (e.g. gender, age, experience). As opposed to **situational variables** which are characteristics of the situation (e.g. hot day, crowded room, distractions).

Order effects come about when participants are tested more than once – as in repeated measures designs. This might lead to better performance through practice, or worse performance due to boredom or fatigue.

Trevor and Mervyn are often mistaken for identical twins – but incredibly, there is an 11-year age gap.

Revision BOOSTER

Remember that even though, in a matched pairs design, there has been some attempt to control for participant variables, there are inevitably differences (even between identical twins), so participant variables may still be a problem.

Knowledge Check

1. Explain what is meant by 'directional hypothesis'. State when a researcher would use a directional hypothesis rather than a non-directional hypothesis. *(3 marks)*

2. Explain the difference between an extraneous and a confounding variable. *(2 marks)*

3. Outline what is meant by 'investigator effects'. Explain why these should be controlled in a research study. *(2 marks + 2 marks)*

4. Give **one** reason why a researcher may choose to use a repeated measures design rather than an independent groups design. *(2 marks)*

Types of experiment

Spec spotlight

Types of experiment, laboratory and field experiments; natural and quasi-experiments.

Apply it

Identify the type of experiment (lab, field, natural or quasi) described below. *(1 mark each)*

1. Investigating whether older people (over 50) or younger people (under 30) are more likely to binge-drink alcohol.

2. Comparing the number of 'treats' received on Halloween by children dressed in 'scary' costumes or in everyday clothes.

3. Measuring how many words from a list people could remember when presented with cues such as category names.

4. Measuring the change in stress levels of people in an affected area before and after an earthquake.

Ben had been stood there for four-and-a-half hours. It was only then he realised that he may have misunderstood his psychology teacher's suggestion that he go out and perform a field experiment.

Laboratory experiment

A controlled environment where **extraneous** and **confounding variables** (EVs and CVs) can be regulated.

Participants go to researcher.

The **IV** is manipulated and the effect on the **DV** is recorded.

⊕ EVs and CVs can be controlled.	This means that the effect of EVs and CVs on the DV can be minimised.	Cause and effect between the IV and DV can be demonstrated (high **internal validity**).
⊕ Can be more easily **replicated**.	Greater control means less chance that new EVs introduced.	This means that findings can be confirmed, supporting their **validity**.
⊖ May lack **generalisability**.	The controlled lab environment may be rather artificial and participants are aware they are being studied.	Thus behaviour may not be 'natural' and can't be generalised to everyday life (low **external validity**).
⊖ **Demand characteristics** may be a problem.	These are cues in the experimental situation that invite a particular response from participants.	The findings may be explained by these cues rather than the effect of the IV (lower internal validity).

Field experiment

A natural setting.

The researcher goes to participants.

The IV is manipulated and the effect on the DV is recorded.

⊕ More natural environment.	Participants more comfortable and behaviour more authentic.	Results may be more generalisable to everyday life.
⊕ Participants are unaware of being studied.	They are more likely to behave as they normally do so the findings can be generalised.	The study has greater external validity.
⊖ More difficult to control CVs/EVs.	Observed changes in the DV may not be due to the IV, but to CVs/EVs instead.	It is more difficult to establish cause and effect than in the lab.
⊖ There are ethical issues.	Participants in a field experiment may not have given **informed consent**.	This is an invasion of participants' privacy, which raises ethical issues.

Natural experiment

The experimenter does not manipulate the IV – it does change, but the change is not made by the experimenter – someone or something else causes the IV to vary. The IV would have varied even if the experimenter wasn't interested.

DV may be naturally occurring (e.g. exam results) or may be devised by the experimenter and measured in the field or a lab.

⊕ May be the only practical/ ethical option.	It may be unethical to manipulate the IV, e.g. studying the effects of institutionalisation on children.	A natural experiment may be the only way causal research can be done for such topics.
⊕ Greater external validity.	Natural experiments involve real-world issues, such as the effect of a natural disaster on stress levels.	This means the findings are more relevant to real experiences.
⊖ The natural event may only occur rarely.	Many natural events are 'one-offs' and this reduces the opportunity for research.	This may limit the scope for generalising findings to other similar situations.
⊖ Participants are not **randomly allocated**.	The experimenter has no control over which participants are placed in which condition as the IV is pre-existing.	May result in CVs that aren't controlled, e.g. Romanian orphans adopted early may also be the friendlier ones.

Colin's 'natural experiment' had not been well received. Turns out there aren't that many streakers at bowls matches.

Natural experiments are not necessarily natural at all. A study might involve a comparison between football players and rugby players (IV varies 'naturally'). The DV could be an IQ test measured in a controlled lab environment. IQ tests aren't that natural.

Quasi-experiment

IV is based on a pre-existing difference between people, e.g. age or gender. No one has manipulated this variable, it simply exists.

DV may be naturally occurring (e.g. exam results) or may be devised by the experimenter and measured in the field or a lab.

⊕ There is often high control.	Often carried out under controlled conditions and therefore shares some of the strengths of lab experiments.	This means, for example, replication is possible.
⊕ Comparisons can be made between people.	In a quasi-experiment the IV is a difference between people, e.g. people with and without autism.	This means that comparisons between different types of people can be made.
⊖ Participants are not randomly allocated.	The experimenter has no control over which participants are placed in which condition as the IV is pre-existing.	*Participant variables* may have caused the change in the DV acting as a CV.
⊖ Causal relationships not demonstrated.	As with a natural experiment, the researcher does not manipulate/control the IV.	We cannot say for certain that any change in the DV was due to the IV.

Knowledge Check

1. Explain what is meant by a 'field experiment'. *(2 marks)*
2. Explain **one** strength **and one** limitation of a laboratory experiment. *(2 marks + 2 marks)*
3. Explain the difference between a field experiment and a natural experiment. *(4 marks)*
4. State **one** difference between a quasi-experiment and a laboratory experiment. *(2 marks)*
5. Outline **one** strength **and one** weakness of a quasi-experiment. *(4 marks)*

Spec spotlight

Sampling: the difference between population and sample: sampling techniques including: random, systematic, stratified, opportunity and volunteer; implications of sampling techniques, including bias and generalisation.

Revision BOOSTER

It is important to note that 'sampling' is a term that's used in a couple of different ways when discussing research. As well as referring to ways in which participants are selected for studies (as on this spread) it's also a way of 'structuring' data collection in an observation – see 'time sampling' and 'event sampling' on page 117.

Volunteer samples can be unrepresentative as they tend to attract people who are keen, curious and overly helpful. As keen as mustard in fact! Hence the mustard. Keep up.

Population and sample

Population.	The large group of people that a researcher is interested in studying, for example college students from the North West.
Sample.	It is usually not possible to include all members of the population in the study, so a smaller group is selected – the *sample*.
Generalisation.	The sample that is drawn should be representative of the population so **generalisations** can be made.
Bias.	Most samples are biased in that certain groups (e.g. men, students, professionals etc) may be over- or under-represented.

Random sample

Equal chance.	Every person in the target population has an equal chance of being selected.	
How?	Lottery method. All members of the target population are given a number and placed in a hat or computer/phone randomiser used.	
⊕ Potentially unbiased.	This means **CVs/EVs** are controlled.	Enhances **internal validity**.
⊖ Time-consuming and may not work.	Complete list of population is hard to get.	Also some participants may refuse to take part.

Systematic sample

Using a set system.	Participants are selected using a set 'pattern' (sampling frame) e.g. list in alphabetical order.	
How?	Every *n*th person is selected from a list of the target population.	
⊕ Unbiased.	The first item is usually selected at random.	Objective method.
⊖ Time and effort.	A complete list of the population is required.	May as well use random sampling.

Stratified sample

Strata.	Sample reflects proportions of people in certain subgroups (strata) within a population.
How?	Subgroups (or 'strata') are identified, e.g. gender or age groups. The relative percentages of the subgroups in the population are reflected in the sample.

⊕ Representative method.	The characteristics of the target population are represented.	Generalisability more likely than other methods.
⊖ Stratification is not perfect.	Strata cannot reflect all the ways in which people are different.	Complete representation is not possible.

Opportunity sample

Most available.	People who are simply most available, i.e. the ones who are nearest/easiest to obtain.
How?	Ask people nearby, e.g. ask the students in your class to take part or ask people who walk past you at a shopping centre.

⊕ Quick method.	Opportunity sampling is convenient because you just make use of the people who are closest.	This makes it cheaper and one of the most popular sampling methods.
⊖ Inevitably biased.	The sample is unrepresentative of the target population as it is drawn from a very specific area, such as one street in one town.	This means that the findings cannot be generalised.

Volunteer sample

Self-selecting.	In a volunteer sample, participants select themselves.
How?	Advertise. For example, place an advert in a newspaper or ask people to put hands up to volunteer.

⊕ Participants are willing.	Participants have selected themselves and know how much time and effort is involved.	Likely to engage more than people stopped in the street.
⊖ Volunteer bias.	Participants may share certain traits, e.g. want to be helpful.	Respond to cues and generalisation limited.

The National Lottery – the ultimate random method and a 1 in 14 million chance of winning!

Face facts my friend – it's never gonna happen...

Apply it

Two psychologists wanted to study caregiver–child interactions using the Strange Situation. They needed to recruit 50 caregivers (and their babies), and decided to use random sampling.

1. Explain how they could obtain a random sample of caregivers from their local area. *(3 marks)*

2. Another psychologist points out that it would be easier to use a volunteer sample. Explain why. *(2 marks)*

3. Explain why volunteer sampling would probably produce a biased sample. *(2 marks)*

Knowledge Check

1. Explain the difference between a population **and** a sample. *(2 marks)*

2. Explain what is meant by 'random sampling'. *(2 marks)*

3. Outline **one** strength **and one** limitation of systematic sampling. *(2 marks +2 marks)*

4. Explain how you could select a stratified sample of students of different ages within a school or college. *(3 marks)*

5. Using an example, explain the implications of using an opportunity sample. *(4 marks)*

Ethical issues and ways of dealing with them

Spec spotlight

Ethics, including the role of the British Psychological Society's code of ethics; ethical issues in the design and conduct of psychological studies; dealing with ethical issues in research.

Apply it

A researcher investigated the effectiveness of a new anti-depressant drug. She randomly allocated participants diagnosed with depression to a treatment group (the new drug) or a control group (a placebo).

1. Explain **two** ethical issues that could have arisen in this study.
   (2 marks + 2 marks)

2. Outline how the psychologist could have dealt with each issue.
   (2 marks + 2 marks)

Knowledge Check

1. Using an example from research into social influence, explain what is meant by 'ethical issue'. *(3 marks)*

2. Identify **one** ethical issue in psychological research. Outline **one** way in which this issue can be dealt with.
   (1 mark + 2 marks)

3. Outline the role of the British Psychological Society's code of ethics in psychological research. *(4 marks)*

Ethical issues

Conflict.	When a conflict exists between the rights of participants and the aims of the research.	*BPS code of conduct* is a quasi-legal document to protect participants based on four principles: *respect, competence, responsibility* and *integrity*. *Ethics committees* weigh up costs (e.g. potential harm) and benefits (e.g. value of research) before deciding whether a study should go ahead.

Informed consent

Get permission.	Issue: Informed judgement about whether to take part. But may reveal aims.	Sign consent form, where appropriate seek parental consent, alternative forms of consent are: • *Presumptive* – ask a similar group. • *Prior general* – agree to be deceived. • *Retrospective* – get consent after the study.

Deception

Misleading.	Issue: Deliberately misleading or withholding information so consent is not informed. But mild deception OK.	At the end of a study, participants should be given a *debrief* where they are advised of: • The true aims of the investigation. • Details that were not given during the study, e.g. existence of other groups or conditions. • What their data will be used for. • Their right to withhold data.

Protection from harm

Risk.	Issue: Participants should be at no more risk than they would be in everyday life.	• Should be given the *right to withdraw* at each stage of the research process. • Should be reassured that their behaviour was typical/normal during the debriefing. • Researcher should provide *counselling* if participants have been, e.g. distressed.

Privacy and confidentiality

Right to control.	Issue: We have the right to control information about ourselves. If this is invaded, confidentiality should be respected.	• If personal details are held these must be protected (a legal requirement). Usually no personal details are recorded. • Researchers refer to participants using numbers, initials or false names. • Participants' personal data cannot be shared with other researchers.

Correlations

Correlation.	Illustrates the strength and direction of an association between two co-variables.
Scattergram.	One co-variable is on the *x*-axis, the other is on the *y*-axis.
Types of correlation.	• *Positive correlation* – co-variables increase together. • *Negative correlation* – one co-variable increases, the other decreases. • *Zero correlation* – no relationship between variables. 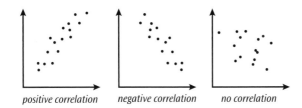 *positive correlation* *negative correlation* *no correlation*
Difference between correlations and experiments.	In an experiment the researcher manipulates the **IV** and records the effect on the **DV**. In a correlation there is no manipulation of variables and so *cause and effect* cannot be demonstrated.
⊕ Useful starting point for research.	By assessing the strength and direction of a relationship, correlations provide a measure of how two variables are related.	If variables are strongly related it may suggest hypotheses for future research.
⊕ Relatively economical.	Unlike a lab study, there is no need for a controlled environment and can use secondary data (e.g. government statistics).	So correlations are less time-consuming than experiments.
⊖ No cause and effect.	Correlations are often presented as causal, e.g. by the media, when they only show how two variables are related.	This leads to false conclusions about causes of behaviour.
⊖ Intervening variables.	Another untested variable may explain relationship between co-variables.	This may also lead to false conclusions.

Spec spotlight

Correlations. Analysis of the relationship between co-variables. The difference between correlations and experiments. Positive, negative and zero correlations.

Apply it

A psychologist investigated a disorder known as seasonal affective disorder (SAD). He found that as the number of daylight hours increased in the spring, participants in the study became less depressed.

Is this a positive, negative or zero correlation? Explain your answer.
(2 marks)

There is apparently a strong positive correlation between the number of ice creams eaten on a particular day and the number of cases of drowning.

Are ice creams that dangerous?! Or could there be a third 'intervening' variable? Hmm.

Knowledge Check

1. Give **two** reasons why a researcher may conduct a correlational study rather than an experiment.
   (2 marks + 2 marks)

2. Explain **one** difference between a correlation and an experiment. *(2 marks)*

3. Explain **one** strength **and one** limitation of using correlations in psychological research. *(2 marks + 2 marks)*

Spec spotlight

Observational techniques. Types of observation: naturalistic and controlled observation; covert and overt observation; participant and non-participant observation.

Observational design: behavioural categories; event sampling; time sampling.

Several of Benedict's fellow researchers had pointed out that his covert observation disguise wasn't quite as brilliant as he thought it was.

Apply it

A psychologist studying stages of attachment observed babies in their own homes. He was especially interested in how much stranger anxiety the babies showed in response to his presence.

1. Explain how this observation study could be described as
   (a) naturalistic, (b) overt and
   (c) participant observation.
   (2 marks + 2 marks + 2 marks)

2. Outline **one** strength **and one** limitation of this study as a naturalistic observation.
   (2 marks + 2 marks)

3. Identify **two** behavioural categories the psychologist could use to measure stranger anxiety.
   (1 mark + 1 mark)

4. Explain how the psychologist could have used time sampling in this study. *(2 marks)*

Observational techniques

A way of seeing or listening to what people do without having to ask them. Observation is often used within an experiment as a way of assessing the **DV**.

⊕ Capture what people do.	People often act differently from how they say they will in self-report methods.	Observations are useful as they give insight into spontaneous behaviour.
⊖ Risk of observer bias.	Researcher's interpretation of the situation may be affected by expectations.	Bias can be reduced using more than one observer.

Naturalistic – takes place where the target behaviour would normally occur.

⊕ High **external validity**.	In a natural context, behaviour is likely to be more spontaneous.	More **generalisable** to everyday life.
⊖ Low control.	There may be uncontrolled **CVs/EVs**.	Makes it more difficult to detect patterns.

Controlled – some control/manipulation of variables including control of CVs/EVs.

⊕ Can be **replicated**.	More easily repeated due to **standardised** procedures.	Findings can be checked to see if they occur again.
⊖ May have low external validity.	Behaviour may be contrived as a result of the setting.	Findings cannot be applied to everyday experience.

Covert – participants are unaware they are being studied.

⊕ **Demand characteristics** reduced.	Participants do not know they are being watched so their behaviour will be more natural.	This increases the **internal validity** of the findings.
⊖ Ethically questionable.	People may not want behaviour recorded, even in public.	Participants' right to privacy may be affected.

Overt – participants are aware of being studied.

⊕ More ethically acceptable.	Participants have given their consent to be studied.	They have the right to withdraw if they wish.
⊖ Demand characteristics.	Knowledge of being studied influences behaviour.	Reduces the internal validity of the findings.

Participant observation – researcher becomes part of group they are studying.

| ⊕ Can lead to greater insight. | Researcher experiences the situation as the participants do. | This enhances the external validity of the findings. |
| ⊖ Possible loss of objectivity. | The researcher may identify too strongly with those they are studying ('going native'). | This threatens the objectivity and internal validity of the findings. |

Non-participant observation – researcher remains separate from the group they are studying.

| ⊕ More objective. | Researcher maintains an objective distance so less chance of bias. | May increase the internal validity of the findings. |
| ⊖ Loss of insight. | Researcher may be too far removed from those they are studying. | May reduce the external validity of the findings. |

Observational design

Behavioural categories – the target behaviour to be observed should be broken up into a set of observable categories. This is similar to *operationalisation*.

| ⊖ Difficult to make clear and unambiguous. | Categories should be self-evident and not overlap, not always possible to achieve. | 'Smiling' and 'grinning' would be poor categories. |
| ⊖ Dustbin categories. | All forms of behaviour should be in the list and not one 'dustbin'. | 'Dumped' behaviours go unrecorded. |

Event sampling – a target behaviour/event is recorded every time it occurs.

| ⊕ Useful for infrequent behaviour. | The researcher will still 'pick up' behaviours that do not occur at regular intervals. | Such behaviours could easily be missed using time sampling. |
| ⊖ Complex behaviour oversimplified. | If the event is too complex, important details may go unrecorded. | This may affect the **validity** of the findings. |

Time sampling – observations are made at regular intervals, e.g. once every 15 seconds.

| ⊕ Reduces the number of observations. | Rather than recording everything that is seen (i.e. continuous) data is recorded at certain intervals. | The observation is more structured and systematic. |
| ⊖ May be unrepresentative. | The researcher may miss important details outside of the timescale. | May not reflect the whole behaviour. |

That'll be a non-participant observation then.

Unstructured observation – everything is recorded which can be quite difficult if a lot is going on.

Structured observation includes behavioural categories and sampling methods.

A naturalistic observation often uses structured design.

Revision BOOSTER

In an observational study, the researcher decides:

- *Who* to sample using sampling methods such as volunteer or opportunity.
- *How* the behaviours are sampled using time or event sampling.

For example, observing whether male or female drivers are more likely to 'jump' a red light would most likely involve opportunity and then event sampling.

Knowledge Check

1. Outline the difference between naturalistic and controlled observation. *(2 marks)*
2. Explain what is meant by 'covert observation'. *(2 marks)*
3. Explain why a researcher may choose to use a covert observation rather than an overt observation. *(2 marks)*
4. Explain **one** strength **and one** limitation of participant observation. *(2 marks + 2 marks)*

Self-report techniques

Spec spotlight

Self-report techniques: questionnaires; interviews, structured and unstructured

Questionnaire construction, including use of open and closed questions; design of interviews.

All self-report techniques are used to assess what people think and/ or feel.

Many questionnaires make use of **rating scales** where respondents are asked to indicate how strongly they feel about a particular topic or issue (perhaps on a scale of 1 to 7) or through a set of verbal designations, such as strongly agree, agree, undecided, disagree, strongly disagree (called a **Likert scale**).

As the only interviewee, Norma felt she had an excellent chance of getting the job. Unfortunately – as would become all too clear six hours later – she had turned up on the wrong day.

There is a danger of **interviewer bias** in interviews. The interviewer may be more likely to encourage the interviewee to explore certain topics when the interaction is 'free-flowing'. This is why most interviews benefit from a clearly defined **interview schedule** (see facing page).

Also, at the analysis stage, the conclusions that are drawn may be due to the subjective (biased) interpretation of the researcher.

Questionnaires

Questionnaires are made up of a pre-set list of written questions (or items) to which a participant responds.

They can be used as part of an *experiment* to assess the **DV**.

⊕ Can be distributed to lots of people.	Gather large amounts of data quickly and researcher need not be present when completed.	Reduces the effort involved and makes questionnaires cost-effective.
⊕ Straightforward to analyse.	Especially if closed, fixed-choice questions are used.	Statistical data can easily be converted to graphs and charts for comparison.
⊖ Responses may not always be truthful.	Respondents tend to present themselves in a positive light.	Thus social desirability bias is possible.
⊖ Response bias.	Respondents may favour a particular kind of response, e.g. they always agree.	This means that all respondents tend to reply in a similar way.

Interviews

Face-to-face or online interaction between an interviewer and interviewee.

Structured interview – list of pre-determined questions asked in a fixed order.

⊕ Easy to **replicate**.	Straightforward to replicate because of **standardised** format.	The format also reduces differences between interviewers.
⊖ Interviewers cannot elaborate.	Interviewers cannot deviate from the topic or explain their questions.	This may limit the richness of data collected.

Unstructured interview – no set questions, there is a general topic to be discussed but the interaction is free-flowing and the interviewee is encouraged to elaborate.

⊕ There is greater flexibility.	Unlike a structured interview, points can be followed up as they arise.	More likely to gain insight into interviewee's worldview and collect unexpected information.
⊖ Increased risk of interviewer bias.	Closer dialogue between interviewer and interviewee.	Means more opportunity for unconcious cues.

Semi-structured interviews – list of questions that have been worked out in advance but interviewers ask further questions based on previous answers.

Designing questionnaires

Writing good questions.	• Avoid jargon: *Do you agree that maternal deprivation in infanthood inevitably leads to affectionless psychopathy?*
	• Avoid double-barrelled questions: *Do you agree that footballers are overpaid and should give 20% of their wages to charity?*
	• Avoid leading questions: *Do you agree that boxing is barbaric?*

Closed questions – respondent has limited choices.

Data produced tends to be *quantitative*, e.g. *How many cigarettes do you smoke a day?* 0–10, 11–20, 21–30, 30+
But can produce *qualitative* data, e.g. *Do you smoke? Yes/No*, and then convert to quantitative.

⊕ Easier to analyse.	Can produce graphs and charts for comparison.	Makes it easier to draw conclusions.
⊖ Responses are restricted.	Forced into an answer that may not represent true feelings.	May reduce the **validity** of the findings.

Open questions – respondent provides own answers expressed in words.

Data produced tends to be qualitative, e.g. *Why did you start smoking?* This question would produce a range of personal answers.

⊕ Responses not restricted.	Answers more likely to provide detailed, unexpected information.	Likely to have more **external validity** than statistics.
⊖ Difficult to analyse.	Wider variety of answers than produced by closed questions.	May be forced to reduce data to statistics.

Designing interviews

Interview schedule.	A standardised list of questions that the interviewer needs to cover, can reduce interviewer bias.
Quiet room.	Will increase the likelihood that the interviewee will open up.
Rapport.	Begin with neutral questions to make participants feel relaxed.
Ethics.	Remind interviewees that answers will be treated in confidence.

The aims and use of piloting

Used in all types of research.

Trial run.	A pilot study is a small-scale trial run of a research design (procedure, questionnaires etc) using a small number of participants.
Aim of piloting.	To find out if certain things don't work so you can correct them before spending time and money on the real thing.

A researcher wanted to investigate the types and severity of people's phobias. She considered using a questionnaire to collect the responses.

1. Write **one** open **and one** closed question the psychologist could use to collect her data.
   (2 marks + 2 marks)

2. Outline **one** strength **and one** limitation of using a questionnaire in this study.
   (2 marks + 2 marks)

3. The researcher decided to conduct interviews instead. Outline **two** issues she should take into account when designing the interview.
   (2 marks + 2 marks)

Knowledge Check

1. Outline what is meant by a 'self-report technique'. *(2 marks)*

2. Explain what is meant by an 'unstructured interview'. *(2 marks)*

3. Outline **one** strength **and one** limitation of using structured interviews. *(2 marks + 2 marks)*

4. Briefly evaluate the use of questionnaires in psychological research. *(4 marks)*

Pilot studies

Spec spotlight

Pilot studies and the aims of piloting.

Knowledge Check

1. Explain the purpose of using a pilot study in psychological research. *(2 marks)*

Types of data

Spec spotlight

Qualitative and quantitative data; the distinction between qualitative and quantitative data collection techniques.

Primary and secondary data, including meta-analysis.

Apply it

A developmental psychologist asks fathers from different cultures to describe their experiences of being a parent. The psychologist also collects relevant data from online sources.

1. Explain **one** strength **and one** limitation of collecting qualitative data in this study.
   (2 marks + 2 marks)

2. Give **one** example of relevant quantitative data the psychologist could have collected. *(1 mark)*

3. Identify the primary **and** secondary data in this study. Explain your answer. *(4 marks)*

Primary data is sometimes called 'field research'. No, come back Ben, it's not what you think!

Knowledge Check

1. Explain what is meant by 'qualitative data'. *(2 marks)*

2. Outline **one** strength **and one** limitation of collecting secondary data in psychological research. *(2 marks + 2 marks)*

3. Referring to an example, briefly discuss the use of meta-analysis in psychology. *(6 marks)*

Qualitative and quantitative data

Qualitative data – *non-numerical* data expressed in words, e.g. extract from a diary.

⊕ Richness of detail.	Much broader in scope than quantitative data.	More meaningful, greater **external validity**.
⊖ Difficult to analyse.	Hard to identify patterns and make comparisons.	Leads to subjective interpretation and researcher bias.

Quantitative data – *numerical* data, e.g. reaction time or number of mistakes.

⊕ Easier to analyse.	Can draw graphs and calculate averages.	So comparisons between groups can be made.
⊖ Narrower in meaning.	Expresses less detail than qualitative data.	Lower external validity – may be less like 'real life'.

Primary and secondary data, including meta-analysis

Primary data – 'first-hand' data collected for the purpose of the investigation.

⊕ Fits the job.	Study designed to extract only the data needed.	Information is directly relevant to research aims.
⊖ Requires time and effort.	Designing and collating questionnaires takes time and expense.	Secondary data can be accessed within minutes.

Secondary data – collected by someone other than the person who is conducting the research, e.g. work of other psychologists or government statistics.

⊕ Inexpensive.	The desired information may already exist.	Requires minimal effort making it inexpensive.
⊖ Quality may be poor.	Information may be outdated or incomplete.	Challenges the **validity** of any conclusions.

Meta-analysis – a type of secondary data that involves combining data from a large number of studies. Calculation of *effect size*.

⊕ Increases validity of conclusions.	The eventual sample size is much larger than individual samples.	Increases the extent to which **generalisations** can be made.
⊖ Publication bias.	Researchers may not select all relevant studies, leaving out negative or non-significant results.	Therefore conclusions may lack validity.

Measures of central tendency and dispersion

Measures of central tendency

Mean – arithmetic average, add up all the scores and divide by the number of scores.

⊕ Sensitive measure.	Includes all the scores/values in the data set within the calculation.	Repesents data set better than median or mode.
⊖ May be unrepresentative.	One very large or small number makes it distorted.	The median or the mode tend not to be so easily distorted.

Median – middle value, place scores in ascending order and select middle value. If there are two values in the middle, the mean of these is calculated.

⊕ Less affected by extreme scores.	The median is only focused on the middle value.	In some cases may be more representative of the data set as a whole.
⊖ Less sensitive than the mean.	The actual values of lower and higher numbers are ignored.	Extreme values may be important.

Mode – most frequent or common value, used with categorical/nominal data.

⊕ Relevant to categorical data.	When data is 'discrete', i.e. represented in categories.	Sometimes the mode is the only appropriate measure.
⊖ An overly simple measure.	The mode may be at one extreme.	It is not a useful way of describing data when there are many modes.

Measures of dispersion

Range – the difference between highest to lowest value (sometimes 1 is added if values have been rounded up or down).

⊕ Easy to calculate.	Arrange values in order and subtract largest from smallest.	Simple formula, easier than the standard deviation.
⊖ Does not account for the distribution of the scores.	The range does not indicate whether most numbers are closely grouped around the mean or spread out evenly.	The standard deviation is a much better measure of dispersion in this respect.

Standard deviation – measure of the average spread around the mean. The larger the standard deviation, the more spread out the data is.

⊕ More precise than the range.	Includes all values within the calculation.	Therefore more accurate picture of the overall distribution of data set.
⊖ It may be misleading.	Can be distorted by extreme values.	Also, extreme values may not be revealed, unlike with the range.

Spec spotlight

Descriptive statistics: measures of central tendency – mean, median, mode; measures of dispersion – range and standard deviation; calculation of range.

Ways of **describing** a set of data include measures of central tendency and dispersion, and also graphs (see next spread).

Apply it

A psychologist investigated the effect of chunking on the capacity of short-term memory. Participants who used chunking recalled a mean of 14.2 letters from a list, with a standard deviation of 6.7. Participants who did not use chunking recalled a mean of 7.5 letters, with a standard deviation of 1.3.

1. What conclusion can you draw from the means in this study?
(2 marks)

2. What conclusion can you draw from the standard deviations in this study? (2 marks)

The number of people who support Man City or Man United in a particular class would be an example of **categorical data** – people can only be in one category or the other.

No, you can't be both!!

Knowledge Check

1. Explain what is meant by 'measure of central tendency'. (2 marks)
2. Explain how a researcher might calculate the mean. (2 marks)
3. Outline **one** strength **and one** limitation of standard deviation as a measure of dispersion. (2 marks + 2 marks)

Presentation of quantitative data

Spec spotlight

Presentation and display of quantitative data: graphs, tables, scattergrams, bar charts, histograms.

Distributions: normal and skewed distributions; characteristics of normal and skewed distributions.

Histogram showing percentage scores in a maths test.

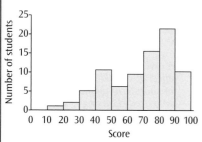

A 'distribution' is a graph showing frequency data. Below is a normal distribution and below right are two types of skewed distributions.

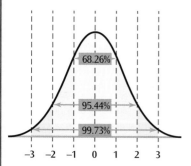

Knowledge Check

1. Explain when a scattergram should be used instead of other types of graphs. *(2 marks)*

2. Describe **two** features of a normal distribution. *(2 marks + 2 marks)*

3. Explain the difference between a normal and skewed distribution. Use an example in your answer. *(4 marks)*

Tables and graphs

Tables.   Raw scores displayed in columns and rows.

A summary paragraph beneath the table explains the findings and draws conclusions.

	SpeedUpp condition	Water condition
Mean	119	96
Standard deviation	53.8	35.8

Bar charts.   Categories (discrete data) are usually placed along the x-axis and frequency on the y-axis (or can be reversed).

The height of each column represents the frequency of that item.

Histograms.   Bars touch each other (in a bar chart they don't) – data is continuous rather than discrete. There is a true zero.

Scattergrams.   Used for correlational analysis. Each dot represents one pair of related data (see page 115). Illustrates strength and direction of correlation.

The data on both axes must be continuous.

Distributions

Normal distribution – symmetrical, bell-shaped curve. Most items are in the middle area of the curve with very few at the extreme ends.

The mean, median and mode all occupy the same mid-point of the curve.

Skewed distributions – distributions that lean to one side or the other because most items are either at the lower or upper end of the distribution.

Negative skew

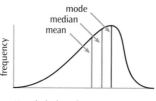

Negatively skewed (longer tail to the left, in a negative direction)

Most of the distribution is concentrated towards the right of the graph, resulting in a long tail on the left.

E.g. a very easy test in which most people get high marks would produce a negative skew.

The mode is the highest point of the peak, the median comes next, and the mean is dragged across to the left (if scores are arranged from lowest to highest).

Positive skew

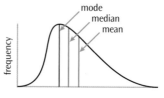

Positively skewed (longer tail to the right, in a positive direction)

Most of the distribution is concentrated towards the left of the graph, resulting in a long tail on the right.

E.g. a very difficult test in which most people get low marks would produce a positive skew.

The mode is the highest point of the peak, the median comes next, and the mean is dragged across to the right (if scores are arranged from lowest to highest).

Mathematical content

Percentages.	Percentage means 'divide by 100'.
Percentage to a decimal.	1. Remove the % sign. 2. Move the decimal point two places to the left.
Decimal places.	Number of digits to the right of the decimal point. Example: 0.0045 is 4 decimal places.
Decimal to a fraction.	1. Work out the number of decimal places in your number. 2. If there are two decimal places then the denominator is 100, three decimal places then the denominator is 1000, etc. 3. Reduce the fraction by finding the highest common factor: the biggest number that divides evenly into both parts of the fraction.
Ratios.	Expressed as *part-to-part ratios* or *part-to-whole ratios*. Should always be divided by the highest common factor. Example: The number of people who support Man City in a class of 20 students = 12. The number who support Man United = 8. • Part-to-part ratio = 12:8 = 3:2 • Part-to-whole ratio (for City fans) = 12:20 = 3:5
Significant figures.	A way to simplify very large or very small numbers by replacing some digits with a zero. Example: The percentage chance that a Man City and Man United fan will get on well = 0.002473691 • To 1 significant figure = 0.002 (3 decimal places). Note that we don't count the zeroes as significant figures. • To 2 significant figures = 0.0025 • 23,450 to 2 significant figures = 23,000 (no decimal places)
Standard form.	Another way of expressing very large or very small numbers. The rule is [number between 1 and 10] $\times$ 10$^{\text{[to the power of x]}}$ 3.2×10^5 is 320,000 (move decimal point 5 places to right) 3.2×10^{-5} is 0.000032 (move decimal point 5 places to left)
Estimates and order of magnitude calculations.	Estimates – give a number to just 1 or 2 significant figures. Order of magnitude – calculate standard form and compare exponents.
Substituting values.	You are given an equation, such as $a = b + c$ You are given values for b and c ($b = 4$ and $c = 7$) What is a? (answer: $a = 11$)

Symbol	Symbol name	Meaning / definition	Example
=	equals sign	equality	$4 = 3 + 1$
>	strict inequality	greater than	$3 > 2$
<	strict inequality	less than	$2 < 3$
>>	inequality	much greater than	$3000 >> 0.02$
<<	inequality	much less than	$0.02 << 3000$
$\propto$	proportional to	proportional to	$f(x) \propto g(x)$
$\approx$	approximately equal	weak approximation	$11 \approx 10$

Spec spotlight

The exam body OFQUAL requires that A level psychology students can:
· Recognise and use expressions in decimal and standard form.
· Use ratios, fractions and percentages.
· Estimate results.
· Use an appropriate number of significant figures.
· Find arithmetic means.
· Construct and interpret frequency tables and diagrams, bar charts and histograms.
· Understand simple probability.
· Understand the principles of sampling as applied to scientific data.
· Understand the terms mean, median and mode.
· Use a scattergram to identify a correlation between two variables.
· Use a statistical test.
· Make order of magnitude calculations.
· Distinguish between levels of measurement.
· Know the characteristics of normal and skewed distributions.
· Select an appropriate statistical test.
· Use statistical tables to determine significance.
· Understand measures of dispersion, including standard deviation and range.
· Understand the differences between qualitative and quantitative data.
· Understand the difference between primary and secondary data.
· Understand and use the symbols: =, <, <<, >>, >, $\propto$, ~.
· Substitute numerical values into algebraic equations using appropriate units for physical quantities.
· Solve simple algebraic equations.
· Translate information between graphical, numerical and algebraic forms.
· Plot two variables from experimental or other data.

Knowledge Check

1. Jimi indicated on a checklist of 20 compulsive behaviours that he had 14 of them. Express Jimi's score as (a) a percentage, (b) a decimal, and (c) a fraction of the total score.
   (1 mark + 1 mark + 1 mark)

2. Pi is 3.141592653, etc. Express this (a) to three decimal places, and (b) to two significant figures.
   (1 mark + 1 mark)

Statistical testing: The sign test

Spec spotlight

Introduction to statistical testing; the sign test. When to use the sign test; calculation of the sign test.

Table of critical values for the sign test.

Level of significance for a **one-tailed test**	0.05	0.025	0.01	0.005
Level of significance for a **two-tailed test**	0.10	0.05	0.02	0.01
N = 5	0			
6	0	0		
7	0	0	0	
8	1	0	0	0
9	1	1	0	0
10	1	1	0	0
11	2	1	1	0
12	2	2	1	1
13	3	2	1	1
14	3	2	2	1
15	3	3	2	2
16	4	3	2	2
17	4	4	3	2
18	5	4	3	3
19	5	4	4	3
20	5	5	4	3
25	7	7	6	5
30	10	9	8	7
35	12	11	10	9

Calculated value of S must be EQUAL TO or LESS THAN critical value in this table for significance to be shown.

Knowledge Check

1. Identify the **three** criteria that need to be met for a sign test to be used to analyse data.
   (3 marks)

2. Give **three** pieces of information that are needed to use a table of critical values. *(3 marks)*

3. Imagine you have calculated a sign test. Explain how you would work out whether the value of *S* is significant or not. *(2 marks)*

Statistical testing

Significance.	The difference/association between two sets of data is greater than what would occur by chance, i.e. it is a meaningful result.
	To find out if the difference/association is *significant* we need to use a *statistical test*.
Probability.	Probability (*p*) is about likelihood – how likely it is that a certain event will happen if the null hypothesis were true. The accepted level of probability in psychology is 0.05 (a significance level of 5%). This is the level at which a researcher decides to accept or reject the null hypothesis. (More stringent 1% significance level may be used e.g. testing drug effects.)
	Even though psychologists may find statistically significant differences/relationships within data, they can never find statistical certainties. This is why psychologists use phrases such as 'this suggests', rather than 'this proves'.
Calculated and *critical values*.	The researcher uses a statistical test to produce a *calculated value*.
	The calculated value is compared with a *critical value* to decide whether the result is significant or not.
	The critical values for a particular test are given in a *table of critical values* (see left).
Finding the critical value.	To find the critical value, need to know:
	1. The significance level (usually 0.05 or 5%).
	2. The number of participants in the investigation (the *N* value) or the degrees of freedom (*df*).
	3. Whether the hypothesis is *directional* (one-tailed test) or *non-directional* (two-tailed test).

The sign test

Conditions of use.	Used to analyse the difference in scores between related items, e.g. the same participant is tested twice (repeated measures).
	Can be used with nominal data (or better).
Calculation.	1. The score for condition B is subtracted from condition A to produce the sign of difference (either a plus or a minus).
	2. Add up the numbers of pluses and the number of minuses.
	3. Participants who achieved the same score in condition A and condition B should be disregarded, and deducted from the *N* value.
	4. The *S* value is the total of the less frequent sign.
Critical value.	If *S* is equal to or less than the critical value, then *S* is significant and the null hypothesis is rejected and the alternative hypothesis accepted at the 5% level of certainty.

Peer review

Peer review		
What is it?	Before publication, all aspects of the investigation are scrutinised by experts ('peers') in the field. These experts should be objective and unknown to the researcher.	
Aims of peer review.	• *Funding*: allocate research funding. • *Validation* of the quality and relevance of research. • *Improvements* and amendments are suggested.	
⊕ Protects quality of published research.	Minimises possibility of fraudulent research and means published research is of the highest quality.	Preserves the reputation of psychology as a science and increases the credibility and status of the subject.
⊖ Anonymity may be used to criticise rival research.	A minority of reviewers may use their anonymous status to criticise rival researchers.	Often there is competition for limited research funding so this may be an issue.
⊖ Publication bias.	Tendency for editors of journals to want to publish 'headline-grabbing' findings.	Means that research that does not meet this criterion is ignored (*file drawer problem*).
⊖ Ground-breaking research may be buried.	Reviewers may be much more critical of research that contradicts their own view.	Peer review may slow down the rate of change within scientific disciplines.

Spec spotlight

The role of peer review in the scientific process.

Apply it

Two psychologists are carrying out longitudinal research into the effects of ageing on memory. Several participants have dropped out. One of the psychologists is tempted to make up some results, but the other warns him that this is a bad idea if they want their research to be published in a reputable journal.

With reference to this disagreement, explain why peer review is necessary in psychological research.

Knowledge Check

1. Explain what is meant by 'peer review'. (2 marks)
2. Outline **two** aims of peer review. (4 marks)
3. Briefly discuss the use of peer review in the scientific process. (6 marks)

Psychological research and the economy

Psychological research and the economy	
The findings of psychological research can benefit our financial prosperity.	
Attachment research into the role of the father.	• Recent research has stressed the importance of the father in a child's healthy psychological development. • This may promote more flexible working arrangements in the family. • This means that modern parents are better equipped to contribute more effectively to the economy.
The development of treatment for mental disorders.	• A third of all days off work are caused by mental disorders such as *depression*. • Psychological research into the causes and treatments of mental disorders means that people have access to therapies or psychotherapeutic drugs, such as SSRIs. • People with mental disorders can manage their condition effectively, return to work and contribute to the economy.

Spec spotlight

The implications of psychological research for the economy.

Knowledge Check

1. Using **two** examples, discuss the implications of psychological research for the economy. (8 marks)

Glossary

attrition The loss of participants from a study over time, which is likely to leave a biased sample or a sample that is too small for reliable analysis. **99**

behaviourist A way of explaining behaviour in terms of what is observable and in terms of learning. **56, 70, 72–77, 88, 96**

biological A perspective that emphasises the importance of physical processes in the body such as genetic inheritance and neural function. **70, 78–79, 89, 104–107**

case study A research method that involves a detailed study of a single individual, institution or event. Case studies provide a rich record of human experience but are hard to generalise from. **35, 65**

classical conditioning Learning by association. Occurs when two stimuli are repeatedly paired together – an unconditioned (unlearned) stimulus (UCS) and a new 'neutral' stimulus (NS). The neutral stimulus eventually produces the same response that was first produced by the unconditioned (unlearned) stimulus alone. **56–57, 72, 96–98**

cognitive Refers to the process of 'knowing', including thinking, reasoning, remembering, believing. **12, 22, 45–47, 66, 70–71, 73–78, 88–89, 94–95, 97, 99–103, 106**

collectivist A group of people who place more value on the 'collective' rather than on the individual, and on interdependence rather than on independence. The opposite is true of individualist culture. **11, 51, 62, 87**

confederate An individual in a study who is not a real participant and has been instructed how to behave by the researcher. **10–11, 16, 19, 26, 28**

confounding variable (CV) A kind of EV but the key feature is that a confounding variable varies systematically with the IV. Therefore we can't tell if any change in the DV is due to the IV or the confounding variable. **31, 39, 45, 63, 65, 67, 69, 108–110**

control condition The condition in a repeated measures design that provides a baseline measure of behaviour without the experimental treatment (IV). **38, 108**

control group In an experiment with an independent groups design, a group of participants who receive no treatment. Their behaviour acts as a baseline against which the effect of the independent variable (IV) may be measured. **25, 26, 29, 35, 42, 54, 66, 99, 114**

counterbalancing An attempt to control for the effects of order in a repeated measures design: half the participants experience the conditions in one order, and the other half in the opposite order. **108**

Conditioned response (CR) In classical conditioning, an unconditioned stimulus (UCS) naturally produces the unconditioned response (UCR). The UCS is repeatedly paired with a neutral stimulus (NS) so that eventually the NS produces the UCR which is now called the conditioned response (CR) and the NS becomes a conditioned stimulus (CS). **56, 72, 96, 98**

Conditioned stimulus (CS) See Conditioned response (CR). **56, 72, 96, 98**

demand characteristics Any cue from the researcher or from the research situation that may be interpreted by participants as revealing the purpose of an investigation. This may lead to a participant changing their behaviour within the research situation. **17, 19, 43, 71, 108, 110, 116**

determinism The view that an individual's behaviour is shaped or controlled by internal or external forces rather than an individual's will to do something. **73, 75, 77, 79, 85, 87–89**

dopamine Neurotransmitter that generally has an excitatory effect and is associated with the sensation of pleasure. Unusually high levels are associated with schizophrenia and unusually low levels are associated with Parkinson's disease. **83, 104**

DV Dependent variable. The variable that is measured by the researcher. Any effect on the DV should be caused by the change in the IV. **108–111, 115–116, 118**

EEG Electroencephalograph. A method of detecting activity in the living brain, electrodes are attached to a person's scalp to record general levels of electrical activity. **70**

experimental group The group in an independent groups design containing the independent variable as distinct from the control. **109**

external validity The degree to which a research finding can be generalised to, for example, other settings (ecological validity), other groups of people (population validity) and over time (temporal validity). **27, 31, 51, 77, 110–111, 116–117, 119, 120**

extraneous variable (EV) Any variable, other than the independent variable (IV), that may affect the dependent variable (DV) if it is not controlled. EVs are essentially nuisance variables that do not vary systematically with the IV. **108–110, 112, 116**

fMRI Functional magnetic resonance imaging. A method used to scan brain activity while a person is performing a task. It enables researchers to detect those regions of the brain which are rich in oxygen and thus are active. **70, 79**

free will The notion that humans can make choices and are not determined by internal biological or external forces. **73, 75, 77, 85–86, 89**

generalisation In conditioning, the tendency to transfer a response from one stimulus to another which is quite similar. In relation to research findings, the extent to which findings and conclusions from a particular investigation can be broadly applied to the population. This is possible if the sample of participants is representative of the population. **11, 51, 55–56, 67, 96, 99, 105, 110–113, 116, 120**

hard determinism The view that all behaviour is caused by something (internal or external factors), so free will is an illusion.   **88**

holism An argument or theory which proposes that it only makes sense to study a whole system rather than its constituent parts (which is the reductionist approach).   **87, 89**

humanistic An approach to understanding behaviour that emphasises the importance of subjective experience and each person's capacity for self-determination.   **71, 85–87, 89**

individualist A group of people who value the rights and interests of the individual. This results in a concern for independence and self-assertiveness. People tend to live in small families unlike collectivist societies. This is typical of Western cultures, in contrast to many non-Western cultures that tend to be collectivist.   **11, 62, 87**

informed consent An ethical issue and an ethical guideline in psychological research whereby participants must be given comprehensive information concerning the nature and purpose of the research and their role in it, in order for them to make an informed decision about whether to participate.   **11, 17, 98–99, 110, 114**

internal validity A kind of validity, concerned with what goes on inside a study – the extent to which the researcher is measuring what was intended. In an experiment, this includes the control of variables to ensure that changes in the DV are solely due to the IV.   **15, 17, 19, 43, 67, 110, 112, 116–117**

IV Independent variable. Some aspect of the experimental situation that is manipulated by the researcher – or changes naturally – so the effect on the DV can be measured.   **108–111, 115**

learning approach The explanation of behaviour using the principles of classical and operant conditioning. The view that all behaviour is learned, a position held by behaviourists.   **72–75, 89**

longitudinal Research conducted over a long period of time – months or years.   **52, 66, 69, 125**

meta-analysis The process of combining the findings from a number of studies on a particular topic. The aim is to produce an overall statistical conclusion (the effect size) based on a range of studies. A meta-analysis should not be confused with a *review* where a number of studies are compared and discussed.   **47, 62, 120**

modelling From the observer's perspective, modelling is imitating the behaviour of a role model. From the role model's perspective, modelling is the precise demonstration of a specific behaviour that may be imitated by an observer.   **57, 74–75, 88**

Neutral stimulus (NS) See Conditioned response (CR).   **56, 72, 96**

operant conditioning A form of learning in which behaviour is shaped and maintained by its consequences. Possible consequences of behaviour include positive reinforcement, negative reinforcement or punishment.   **56, 72–73, 75, 88, 96–97**

prefrontal cortex Section of the cerebral cortex at the front of the brain associated with working memory and planning.   **35, 76**

psychodynamic A perspective that describes the different forces (dynamics), most of which are unconscious, that operate on the mind and direct human behaviour and experience.   **22, 71, 84–85, 89**

random allocation An attempt to control for participant variables in an independent groups design which ensures that each participant has the same chance of being in one condition as any other.   **14–15, 108–109, 111, 114**

reliability Refers to how consistent the findings from an investigation or measuring device are. A measuring device is said to be reliable if it produces consistent results every time it is used.   **49, 61**

reductionism The belief that human behaviour is best explained by breaking it down into smaller constituent parts.   **77, 87–89**

replicate The opportunity to repeat an investigation under the same conditions in order to test the validity and reliability of its findings.   **15, 17, 19, 31, 41, 65, 110–111, 116, 118**

serotonin A neurotransmitter found in the central nervous system. Low levels have been linked to many different behaviours and physiological processes, including aggression, eating disorders and depression.   **78–79, 83, 104–107**

social learning theory A way of explaining behaviour that includes both direct and indirect reinforcement, combining learning theory with the role of cognitive factors.   **57, 74–75**

soft determinism The view that behaviour may be predictable (caused by internal/external factors) but there is also room for personal choice from a limited range of possibilities (restricted free will).   **77, 88**

standardised (procedures and instructions) Using exactly the same formalised procedures and instructions for all participants in a research study so as to avoid investigator effects caused by different procedures/instructions.   **70–71, 116, 118–119**

Unconditioned stimulus (UCS) See Conditioned response (CR).   **56, 72, 96, 98**

Unconditioned response (UCR) See Conditioned response (CR).   **56, 72, 96**

validity Refers to whether an observed effect is a genuine one.   **15, 17, 19, 25, 27, 29, 31, 37, 39, 43, 49, 51, 53, 59, 61, 63, 67, 69, 77, 87, 109–112, 116–117, 119–120**

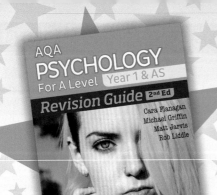